# ANZIO

# BEACHHEAD

## 22 JANUARY – 25 MAY 1944

MILITARY INSTRVCTION

*CENTER OF MILITARY HISTORY*

*UNITED STATES ARMY*

*WASHINGTON, D.C., 1990*

First printed by the Historical Division, War Department,
for the American Forces in Action series, 1948

CMH Pub 100-10

# Foreword to CMH Edition

*Anzio Beachhead (22 January–25 May 1944)* is one of a series of fourteen studies of World War II operations originally published by the War Department's Historical Division and now returned to print as part of the Army's commemoration of the fiftieth anniversary of that momentous clash of arms. These volumes, prepared by professional historians shortly after the events described, provide a concise summary of some of the major campaigns and battles fought by American soldiers. The skillful combination of combat interviews with primary sources, many of which are now lost, gives these unassuming narratives a special importance to military historians. The careful analysis of key operations provides numerous lessons for today's military students.

I am pleased that this entire group of studies will once again be available. I urge all military students and teachers to use them to enhance our collective awareness of the skill, leadership, daring, and professionalism exhibited by our military forebears.

Washington, D.C.                     HAROLD W. NELSON
15 September 1989                    Colonel, FA
                                     Chief of Military History

# FOREWORD

---

*In a nation at war, teamwork by the whole people is necessary for victory. But the issue is decided on the battlefield, toward which all national effort leads. The country's fate lies in the hands of its soldier citizens; in the clash of battle is found the final test of plans, training, equipment, and—above all— the fighting spirit of units and individuals.*

*AMERICAN FORCES IN ACTION SERIES presents detailed accounts of particular combat operations of United States forces. To the American public, this record of high achievement by men who served their Nation well is presented as a preface to the full military history of World War II. To the soldiers who took part in the operations concerned, these narratives will give the opportunity to see more clearly the results of orders which they obeyed and of sacrifices which they and their comrades made, in performance of missions that find their meaning in the outcome of a larger plan of battle.*

DWIGHT D. EISENHOWER
*Chief of Staff*

# DEPARTMENT OF THE ARMY

## Historical Division

## Washington 25, D. C.

## 1 October 1947

*Anzio Beachhead,* fourteenth in the series of studies of particular combat operations, is the story of how VI Corps of the American Fifth Army seized and held a strategic position far to the rear of the main fighting front, in the Italian campaign of 1944. Since VI Corps included British as well as American units, and the high command in Italy was in British rather than in American hands, the battle to maintain the Anzio beachhead was an Allied rather than an exclusively American operation. Essentially, this narrative of Anzio is confined to the first six weeks of bitter struggle to hold the beachhead against German attacks designed to drive the Allied forces from their foothold, a period which ended on 3 March. Thereafter, until the Allied offensive of May, the Anzio beachhead was a static and relatively quiet front. Then the beachhead forces spearheaded the drive that led to the capture of Rome. Only a sketch of this final and decisive phase of the Anzio operation is included in this narrative.

This study is based upon a first narrative by Capt. John Bowditch, III, prepared in the field from military records and from notes and interviews recorded during and after the operation by Captain Bowditch and by 1st Lt. Robert W. Komer. Although as published this book contains no documentation, the original narrative, fully documented, is on file in the War Department. Captain Bowditch's manuscript has been revised and extended with the help of additional information, including that obtained from enemy records, in the Historical Division, War Department Special Staff, by Maj. Roy Lamson, Jr., and by Dr. Stetson Conn. The maps were planned by Col. Allison R. Hartman of the Historical Division, and they were designed and drafted by the World War I Branch of the Division. The photographs were selected by Capt. Robert L. Bodell of the Historical Division. In order that the more definitive history of this operation may be as complete and correct as possible, readers are urged to send all comments, criticisms, and additional data to the Historical Division, Department of the Army, Washington 25, D. C.

# CONTENTS

# Illustrations

# Maps

AFTER THE BATTLE. *The central square of Cisterna, 26 May 1944.*

# THE ANZIO LANDING
## (22–29 January)

In the early morning hours of 22 January 1944, VI Corps of Lt. Gen. Mark W. Clark's Fifth Army landed on the Italian coast below Rome and established a beachhead far behind the enemy lines. In the four months between this landing and Fifth Army's May offensive, the short stretch of coast known as the Anzio beachhead was the scene of one of the most courageous and bloody dramas of the war. The Germans threw attack after attack against the beachhead in an effort to drive the landing force into the sea. Fifth Army troops, put fully on the defensive for the first time, rose to the test. Hemmed in by numerically superior enemy forces, they held their beachhead, fought off every enemy attack, and then built up a powerful striking force which spearheaded Fifth Army's triumphant entry into Rome in June.

The story of Anzio must be read against the background of the preceding phase of the Italian campaign. The winter months of 1943–44 found the Allied forces in Italy slowly battering their way through the rugged mountain barriers blocking the roads to Rome. After the Allied landings in southern Italy, German forces had fought a delaying action while preparing defensive lines to their rear. The main defensive barrier guarding the approaches to Rome was the Gustav Line, extending across the Italian peninsula from Minturno to Ortona. Enemy engineers had reinforced the natural mountain defenses with an elaborate network of pillboxes, bunkers, and mine fields. The Germans had also reorganized their forces to resist the Allied advance. On 21 November 1943, Field Marshal Albert Kesselring took over the command of the entire Italian theater; *Army Group C,* under his command, was divided into two armies, the *Tenth* facing the southern front and also holding the Rome area, and the *Fourteenth* guarding central and northern Italy. In a year otherwise filled with defeat, Hitler was determined to gain the prestige of holding the Allies south of Rome. (Map No. 1.)

Opposing the German forces was the Allied 15th Army Group, commanded by Gen. Sir Harold R. L. G. Alexander, with the U.S. Fifth Army attacking on the western and the British Eighth Army on the eastern sectors of the front. In mid-December, men of the Fifth Army were fighting their way through the forward enemy defensive positions, which became known as the Winter Line.[1]

---

[1]An account of this operation is given in *Fifth Army at the Winter Line* (American Forces in Action Series, Military Intelligence Division, U.S. War Department), Washington, 1945.

THE ANZIO BEACHHEAD TERRAIN, *looking northeast over the flat plain toward Velletri Gap. In the foreground is the town of Anzio. Nettuno is on the right. (Photo taken in September 1944.)*

VELLETRI GAP

LAZIALI

MONTI LEPINI

NETTUNO

ANZIO

Braving the mud, rain, and cold of an unusually bad Italian winter, scrambling up precipitous mountain slopes where only mules or human pack-trains could follow, the Allied forces struggled to penetrate the German defenses. By early January, Fifth Army troops had broken through the Winter Line and had occupied the heights above the Garigliano and Rapido Rivers, from which they could look across to Mount Cassino, with Highway No. 6 curving around its base into the Liri Valley. Before them were the main ramparts of the Gustav Line, guarding this natural corridor to the Italian capital. Buttressed by snow-capped peaks flanking the Liri Valley, and protected by the rain-swollen Garigliano and Rapido Rivers, the Gustav Line was an even more formidable barrier than the Winter Line. Unless some strategy could be devised to turn the defenses of the Gustav Line, Fifth Army faced another long and arduous mountain campaign.

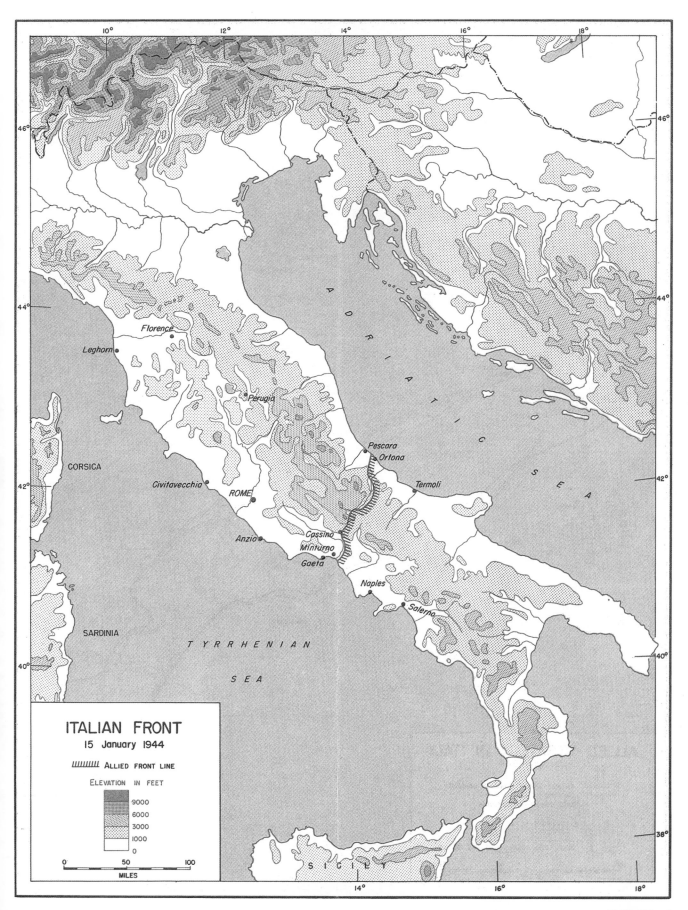

ITALIAN FRONT

15 January 1944

IIIIIIIII ALLIED FRONT LINE

ELEVATION IN FEET

9000
6000
3000
1000
0

0      50      100

MILES

Florence

Leghorn

Perugia

Pescara
Ortona

CORSICA

Civitavecchia

ROME

Termoli

Anzio

Cassino
Minturno

Gaeta

Naples

Salerno

SARDINIA

T Y R R H E N I A N

S E A

A D R I A T I C    S E A

S I C I L Y

MAP NO. 1

ADRIATIC
SEA

Pescara
Chieti
Ortona
Tollo

⬚ 5

2921

⬚ XXX
LXXVI
(Armored)

Casoli

PESCARA R.

SANGRO R.

Papoli

2795

TIBER R.

2487

Callarmele

Avezzano

TENTH ARMY

⬚ XX
305 (+)
Group Hauk

42°                                                                                                      42°

HIGHWAY NO 5

ROME

⬚ XXX
I
Prcht

Valmontone

Colli Laziali

Albano

Velletri

HIGHWAY NO 6

SACCO R.

Lepini
1536 Mt.

Frosinone

⬚ XXX
XIV
(Armored)

⬚ 13

2283

Alfedena

1533

Cassino

RAPIDO R.

⬚ XXX
FEC

LIRI R.

GARIGLIANO R.

EIGHTH BR.
XXX
FIFTH U.S.

⬚ XXX
II

Anzio

Nettuno

HIGHWAY NO 7

Terracina

Gaeta

⬚ XXX
10

VOLTURNO R.

T Y R R H E N I A N     S E A

⬚ XXX
VI

41°                                                                                                      41°

NAPLES

## ALLIED STRATEGY IN ITALY
### January 1944

〰〰〰〰〰  ALLIED FRONT LINE 15 JANUARY
━━━━━  GUSTAV LINE
*Units as of 15 January*

ELEVATIONS IN METERS

0    200   600 1000 1600 and above

10        0            10          20
MILES

13°                                                    14°

*MAP NO. 2*

## Plan for a New Offensive

The strategy decided upon by the Allied leaders, an amphibious landing behind the Gustav Line, had been under consideration from the time when German intentions in Italy became clear. By late October 1943 it was evident that the Germans intended to compel the Allied forces to fight a slow, costly battle up the peninsula. To meet this situation, Allied staffs began to consider a plan for landing behind the enemy lines, with the purpose of turning the German flank, gaining a passage to the routes to Rome, and threatening the enemy lines of communication and supply. On the Eighth Army front, a small-scale amphibious landing at Termoli on 2–3 October 1943 furnished a pattern for such an attack.

On 8 November 1943 General Alexander ordered the Fifth Army to plan an amphibious landing on the west coast. The target date was set at 20 December. The landing, to be made by a single division, was to be the third phase of an over-all operation in Italy. In the first phase the Eighth Army was to carry out an offensive which would put it astride Highway No. 5, running from Pescara on the Adriatic coast through Popoli and Collarmele toward Rome. The second phase would be a Fifth Army drive up the Liri and Sacco Valleys to capture Frosinone. Dependent on the progress of the first two phases, a landing south of Rome directed toward Colli Laziali (the Albanese Mountains) would be made, to link up with the forces from the south. Because of tenacious German opposition and difficult terrain, the Eighth and Fifth Armies in the Winter Line campaign could not reach their assigned objectives. This situation, together with the lack of available landing craft, made the plan for an immediate amphibious end-run impracticable, and the project was abandoned on 20 December 1943.

The slow progress of the Allied advance led to the revival of the plan for an amphibious operation south of Rome along the lines previously contemplated. At Tunis on Christmas Day the chief Allied military leaders drafted new plans for an amphibious landing below Rome with increased forces and the necessary shipping. Two divisions, plus airborne troops and some armor—over twice the force originally planned—were to make the initial assault between 20 and 31 January, but as near 20 January as possible to allow a few days latitude if bad weather should force postponement. The amphibious operation was again to be coordinated with a drive from the south, which would begin earlier. (Map No. 2.)

Main Fifth Army, reinforced by two fresh divisions from the quiescent Eighth Army front, was to strike at the German *Tenth Army* across the Garigliano and Rapido Rivers, breach the Gustav Line, and drive up the Liri Valley. This offensive was planned in sufficient strength to draw in most of the available German reserves. While the enemy was fully occupied in defending the Gustav Line, the surprise landing would be made in his rear at the twin resort towns of Anzio and Nettuno, about thirty miles south of Rome. Once established, the assault force was to thrust inland toward the volcanic heights of Colli Laziali. The capture of Colli Laziali would block vital enemy supply routes and threaten to cut off the German troops holding the Gustav Line. The Allied leaders believed that the Germans lacked sufficient strength to meet attacks on two fronts and that they would be forced to rush troops northward to meet the grave threat to their rear. Thus weakened, the Germans could be forced to withdraw up the Liri Valley from their Gustav Line positions. Eighth Army, though depleted of two divisions which were to go to the Fifth Army front, was to make a show of force along its front in order to contain the maximum number of enemy forces. If possible, Eighth Army would reach Highway No. 5 and develop a threat toward Rome through Popoli by 20 January. Main Fifth Army was to follow up the anticipated enemy withdrawal as quickly as possible, link up with the beachhead force, and drive on Rome.

The area chosen for the amphibious landing was a stretch of the narrow Roman coastal plain extending north from Terracina across the Tiber River. (Map No. 3.) Southeast of Anzio this plain is covered by the famous Pontine Marshes; northwest toward the Tiber it is a region of rolling, often wooded, farm country. The 3,100-foot hill mass of Colli Laziali lies about twenty miles inland from Anzio and guards the southern approaches to Rome. (Map No. 21.) Highway No. 7 skirts the west side of Colli Laziali; on the southeast the mountains fall away into the low Velletri Gap leading inland toward Highway No. 6 at Valmontone. The main west-coast railways parallel these highways. On the east side of the Velletri Gap rise the peaks of the Lepini Mountains which stretch along the inner edge of the Pontine Marshes toward Terracina.

An area roughly seven miles deep by fifteen miles wide around Anzio was to form the initial Allied beachhead. (Map No. 3.) Its 26-mile perimeter was considered the maximum which could be held by the initial assault force and yet include the best natural features for defense. In the sector northwest of Anzio the beachhead was bounded by the Moletta River. Here the low coastal plain was cut up by a series of rough-hewn stream gullies, the largest of them formed by the Moletta and the Incastro Rivers running southwest from the higher ground inland toward the sea. These gullies, though their small streams were easily fordable, were often fifty feet deep and offered difficult obstacles to armor. In the central beachhead sector, east of the first overpass on the Anzio–Albano road, the line ran 6,000 yards across a broad stretch of almost level open fields to meet the west branch

LITTORIA AND THE RIGHT FLANK *of the beachhead, viewed from the air. The Mussolini Canal flows from right to left across the terrain shown in this photo, about one-third of the distance between Littoria and Anzio. The Factory (Aprilia) was very similar in structure, and built about the same time as Littoria.*

TORRE ASTURA

ANZIO

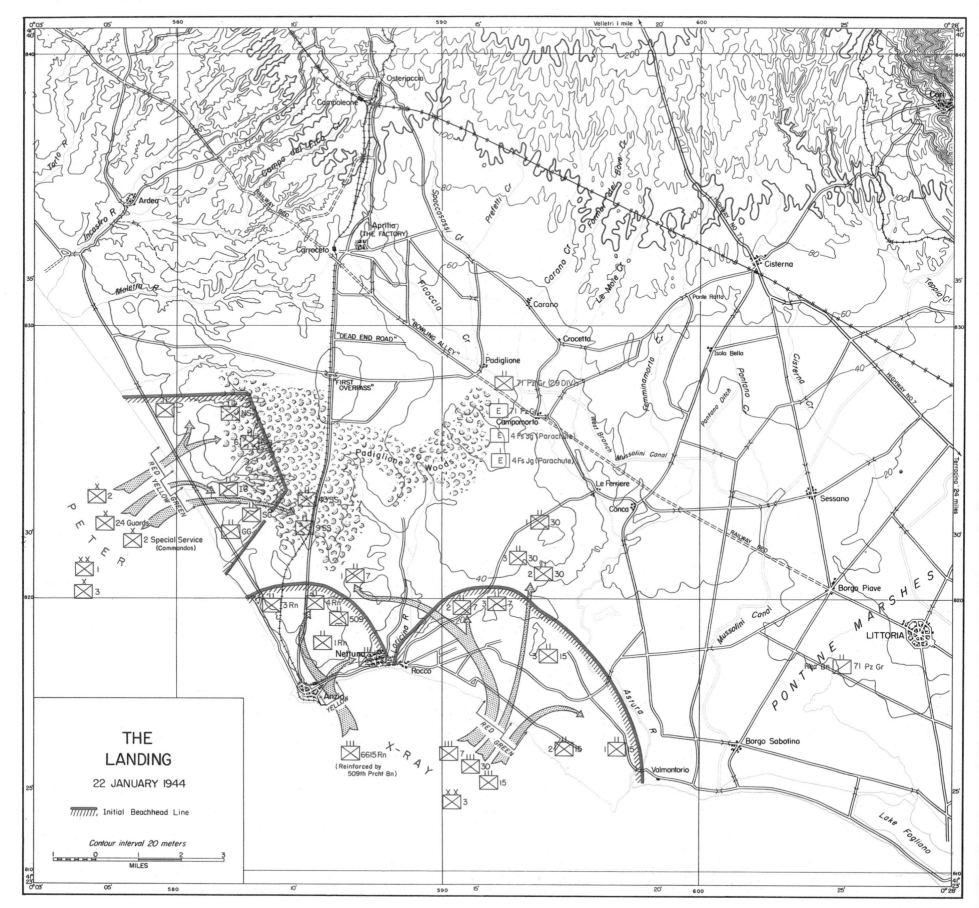

THE
LANDING

22 JANUARY 1944

Initial Beachhead Line

Contour interval 20 meters

MILES

MAP NO. 3

of the Mussolini Canal below the village of Padiglione. This stretch of open country leading inland along the Albano road formed the best avenue of approach into or out of the beachhead and was to be the scene of major Allied and German attacks.

Between Cisterna and Littoria the plain merged with the northern edge of the Pontine Marshes, a low, flat region of irrigated fields interlaced with an intricate network of drainage ditches. The treeless, level expanse offered scant cover for troops, and during the rainy season the fields were impassable to most heavy equipment. From Padiglione east the entire right flank of the initial beachhead line was protected by the Mussolini Canal, which drains the northern edge of the Pontine Marshes. The line ran east along the west branch of the canal to its intersection with the main branch and from there down the main branch to the sea. The canal and the Pontine Marshes made the beachhead right flank facing Littoria a poor avenue of attack; this flank could be held with a minimum of forces.

Most of the beachhead area was within an elaborate reclamation and resettlement project. The low, swampy, malarial bogland of the Pontine Marshes had been converted into an area of cultivated fields, carefully drained and irrigated by an extensive series of canals and pumping stations. Only in the area immediately north of Anzio and Nettuno had the scrub timber, bog, and rolling grazing land been left untouched. At regular intervals along the network of paved and gravel roads crisscrossing the farmlands were the standardized 2-story *podere,* or farmhouses, built for the new settlers. Such places as the new community center of Aprilia, called the "Factory" by Allied troops, and the provincial capital of Littoria, were modernistic model towns. The twin towns of Anzio (ancient Antium) and Nettuno in the center of the beachhead were popular seaside resorts before the war.

The plan for the landing was called SHINGLE. Originally conceived as a subsidiary operation on the left flank of an advancing Fifth Army, it developed, when main Fifth Army failed to break the

MAJ. GEN. JOHN P. LUCAS
*Commanding General, VI Corps*

mountain defenses in the south, into a major operation far in the enemy rear. U.S. VI Corps, selected by General Clark to make the amphibious landing, employed British as well as American forces under the command of Maj. Gen. John P. Lucas. The assault force was to be dispatched from Naples, and was to consist of the U.S. 3d Division, veteran of landings in Sicily and North Africa, the British 1 Division from the Eighth Army front, the 46 Royal Tank Regiment, the 751st Tank Battalion, the 509th Parachute Infantry Battalion, the 504th Parachute Infantry Regiment, Commandos, Rangers, and other supporting troops. This force was the largest that could be lifted by the limited number of landing craft available. It was estimated that the turnaround would require three days. As soon as the convoy returned to Naples, the U.S. 45th Division and the U. S. 1st Armored Division (less Combat Command B), were sent as reinforcements.

The final plans for SHINGLE were completed and approved on 12 January. D Day was set for

22 January; at H Hour (0200), VI Corps was to land over the beaches near Anzio and Nettuno in three simultaneous assaults. On the right, the 3d Division, under Maj. Gen. Lucian K. Truscott, Jr., would land three regiments in assault over X-Ray Red and Green Beaches, two miles below Nettuno.[2] In the center, the 6615th Ranger Force (Provisional) of three battalions, the 83d Chemical Battalion, and the 509th Parachute Infantry Battalion would come in over Yellow Beach, a small beach adjacent to Anzio harbor, with the mission of seizing the port and clearing out any coastal defense batteries there. On Peter Beach, six miles northwest of Anzio, the 2 Brigade Group of the British 1 Division, commanded by Maj. Gen. W. R. C. Penney, would make the assault; the 2 Special Service Brigade of 9 and 43 Commandos would land with it and strike east to establish a road block on the main road leading from Anzio to Campoleone and Albano. All these forces would link up to seize and consolidate a beachhead centering on the port of Anzio. (Map No. 3.)

The assault plan assumed the possibility of initial heavy resistance on the beaches, and the certainty of heavy counterattacks once the enemy was fully aware of the extent of the landing. Consequently, VI Corps held out a strong reserve and placed great emphasis on digging in early at initial objectives to repel armored counterattacks. The bulk of the 1 Division, with the 46 Royal Tank Regiment, the 24 Field Regiment, and the 80 Medium Regiment attached, was to remain on shipboard as a floating reserve. The 504th Parachute Infantry would land behind the 3d Division and also assemble in Corps reserve. Up to a few days before the landing, it had been intended to drop the paratroopers behind the beaches. This drop was called off because its objective was about the same as that of the 1 Division, and because dropping before H Hour might prematurely reveal the main assault. A drop at H Hour itself might

incur the danger of being fired on by Allied artillery if enemy planes should attack at the same time.

The Allied High Command expected that a landing in strength to the rear of *XIV Panzer Corps,* opposing main Fifth Army on the Cassino front, would be considered an emergency to be met by all the resources of the German High Command in Italy. From the latest intelligence available on enemy troops in the Rome area, Army G–2 estimated that VI Corps could expect an initial D Day resistance from one division assigned to coast watching, four parachute battalions from Rome, a tank and an antitank battalion, and miscellaneous coast defense personnel, totaling 14,300 men. By D plus 1, another division, an SS infantry regiment from north of Rome, a regimental combat team from *XIV Panzer Corps* reserve, and perhaps elements of the *Hermann Goering Panzer Division* could arrive. By D plus 2 or 3 the enemy might have appreciated that the Allies had weakened the Eighth Army front; if so, he could bring the *26th Panzer Division* from that sector to produce a total build-up of 31,000 men. If the Fifth Army attack in the south were sufficiently powerful and sustained, it should pin down all enemy reserves in that area. G–2 did not believe that the Germans could bring down reinforcements quickly from northern Italy, especially in the face of overwhelming Allied air superiority. Probable build-up from north of Florence was estimated to be not more than two divisions by D plus 16. The final summary by G–2, Fifth Army, on 16 January pointed out the increasing attrition of enemy troops:

Within the last few days there have been increasing indications that enemy strength on the Fifth Army front is ebbing, due to casualties, exhaustion, and possibly lowering of morale. One of the causes of this condition, no doubt, has been the recent, continuous Allied attacks. From this it can be deduced that he has no fresh reserves and very few tired ones. His entire strength will probably be needed to defend his organized defensive positions.

In view of the weakening of enemy strength on the front as indicated above, it would appear doubtful if the enemy can hold the organized defensive line through

<hr>

[2] *Attached:* 601st Tank Destroyer Battalion; 751st Tank Battalion; 441st AAA Automatic Weapons Battalion; Battery B, 36th Field Artillery Regiment (155-mm. gun); 69th Armored Field Artillery Battalion (105-mm. self-propelled howitzer); and 84th Chemical Battalion (motorized).

PRELOADED SUPPLY TRUCKS AND DUKW's *at Naples on 18 January are loaded aboard LST's. This novel supply method was getting its first Mediterranean battle test in the Anzio beachhead operation.*

Cassino against a co-ordinated army attack. Since this attack is to be launched before Shingle, it is considered likely that this additional threat will cause him to withdraw from his defensive position once he has appreciated the magnitude of that operation.

Whatever the enemy resistance and coast defenses might be, two natural obstacles, bad weather and poor beaches, made a landing at Anzio in January extremely hazardous. The winter rainy season was the worst time of year to launch an amphibious assault. Rain, low clouds, and high seas promised to complicate the problem of supply over the beaches and to hamper air support. The beaches themselves, much shallower than those at Salerno, had the added disadvantage of two offshore sandbars. The Navy estimated that only smaller craft such as LCVP's, LCA's, and DUKW's could be landed with any reasonable

TROOPS FILING ABOARD AT NAPLES *for the invasion were in a happy frame of mind when this picture was taken. A part of the 6615th Ranger Force (Provisional), they were transported to Anzio aboard the stubby LCI's shown in the background.*

hope of success.[3] These risks had to be accepted, although special precautions could be taken to minimize their effect. Since the weather promised only two good days out of seven, the assault convoy was to be combat-loaded for complete discharge within two days; to permit larger craft to unload over the shallow beaches, pontons were to be carried to serve as mobile piers; and to decrease the turnaround time of craft, the novel method of loading LST's with preloaded supply trucks was to be used for the first time in the

Mediterranean Theater. The trucks were to load at Naples, drive onto the LST's, and drive off again at Anzio. It was hoped that the small port of Anzio could be captured before the enemy had time to demolish it. Its capture intact would help to ease the grave problem of supply over open and exposed beaches.

To protect the establishment of the beachhead an elaborate air program in two phases was projected. Prior to D Day the Tactical Air Force would bomb enemy airfields to knock out the German Air Force, and would seek to cut communications between Rome and the north which enemy reinforcements might use. The Strategic Air Force would assist in these tasks. Then, from D Day on, every effort would be made to isolate the beachhead from enemy forces by maintaining air superiority over the beachhead, bombing bridges and road transport, and attacking enemy columns or troop concentrations within striking distance.

---

[3] The naval craft referred to by abbreviations in this and subsequent chapters are identified as follows:

|  |  |
|---|---|
| DUKW | —Amphibious Truck |
| LCA | —Landing Craft, Assault |
| LCI | —Landing Craft, Infantry |
| LCT | —Landing Craft, Tank |
| LCT (R) | —Landing Craft, Tank (Rocket) |
| LCVP | —Landing Craft, Vehicle and Personnel |
| LSI | —Landing Ship, Infantry |
| LST | —Landing Ship, Tank |

For this program much of the strength of the Tactical Air Force would be available, and assistance from other Allied air power in the Mediterranean Theater would be on call. Support would be drawn from some 2,600 Allied aircraft in Italy, Corsica, and Sardinia, representing an overwhelming superiority over available German air power. XII Air Support Command, under Maj. Gen. E. J. House, reinforced by two groups from the Desert Air Force, would provide direct air support, while the Tactical Bomber Force flew heavier missions. The Coastal Air Force would give day and night fighter cover to the mounting area at Naples and halfway up the convoy route. From here on the 64th Fighter Wing would cover the battle area. A total of 60 squadrons (23½ fighter, 6 fighter-bomber, 4 light bomber, 24 medium bomber, and 2½ reconnaissance) would directly support the ground effort. Enemy air power was not considered a major threat. By early January almost the entire long-range bomber force of the *Second German Air Force,* under General Baron von Richthofen, had disappeared from Italian fields. It was believed that Allied attacks on enemy bases would reduce the remaining German air strength by 60 percent. It was not considered likely that the German Air Force would reinforce its units in Italy to meet SHINGLE, so the enemy air effort, never strong, should gradually diminish.

Rear Admiral F. J. Lowry, USN, commander of Task Force 81, was charged with the responsibility of mounting, embarking, and landing the ground forces and with the subsequent support of this force until it was firmly established ashore. His assault convoy numbered 2 command ships, 4 Liberties, 8 LSI's, 84 LST's, 96 LCI's, and 50 LCT's, escorted by cruisers, destroyers, and a host of lesser craft. It was divided into two groups, Task Force X-Ray under Admiral Lowry to lift the American troops, and Task Force Peter under Adm. T. H. Troubridge, RN, for British troops.[4]

Since only sixteen 6-davit LST's were available, the eight LSI's had been assigned to provide additional assault craft. Even with this addition, LCI's would have to be used for follow-up waves over X-Ray Beach. Peter Beach was so shallow that only light assault craft could be used.

Task Force X-Ray was further divided into several functional groups: a control group of two flagships; a sweeper group to clear a mine-free channel; and an escort group for antiaircraft and submarine protection. A beach identification group was designated to precede the assault craft, to locate the beaches accurately, and mark them with colored lights. Then three craft groups would land the assault waves. Following the first wave, the 1st Naval Beach Battalion would improve the marking of beach approaches and control boat traffic. A salvage group was assigned to lay ponton causeways after daylight for unloading heavier craft. Back at Naples a loading control group would handle berthing and loading of craft.

To gain surprise no preliminary naval bombardment of the beaches was ordered, except a short intense rocket barrage at H minus 10 to H minus 5 minutes by three LCT(R)'s. An important assignment, however, was given to a naval task force which was to deliver a feint at H Hour of D Day by bombarding Civitavecchia, north of Rome, and by carrying out dummy landings.

---

[4] The naval craft were assigned as follows:

*Task Force "Peter" (British)*

1 Hq ship
4 cruisers
8 Fleet destroyers
6 Hunt destroyers
2 antiaircraft ships
2 Dutch gunboats
11 fleet mine sweepers
6 small mine sweepers
4 landing craft, gun
4 landing craft, flak
4 landing craft tank (rocket)

*Task Force "X-Ray" (American)*

1 Hq ship
1 cruiser
8 destroyers
2 destroyer escorts
6 mine sweepers
12 submarine chasers (173')
20 submarine chasers (110')
18 motor mine sweepers
6 repair ships

The Germans foresaw the possibility of an Allied landing behind the Gustav Line, and strengthened the coastal positions that were in the most likely invasion areas as best they could with the limited number of troops at their disposal. Since it considered the number of German troops in Italy barely sufficient to hold the southern front and strengthen the rear areas, the German High Command in December 1943 worked out an elaborate plan to reinforce German troops in Italy with units from France, Germany, and Yugoslavia in the event of an Allied landing. Thus it was that while the Germans realized that they did not have available sufficient forces to prevent an Allied landing

behind the Gustav Line, they believed that they could contain and then destroy it by hurrying reinforcements into Italy to meet the emergency. Their plans did not contemplate the withdrawal of any substantial number of troops from the southern front to meet such a threat to their rear.

The bitter and continuous struggle along the southern front from November 1943 into January 1944 forced the enemy to commit all of his divisions that were fit for combat to stop the Allied offensive at the Gustav Line. A lull in the fighting in early January permitted the strengthening of forces in the Rome area to resist an invasion. Under the command of *I Parachute Corps,* the *29th* and

*90th Panzer Grenadier Divisions* were assigned to the Rome coastal sector; the *Herman Goering Panzer Division* was held as a mobile reserve between Rome and the southern front. But when the American Fifth Army attacked across the Garigliano on 18 January, the Germans rushed the *29th* and *90th Panzer Grenadier Divisions* southward. On the eve of the Anzio landing, the Germans had almost denuded the Rome area of combat troops in order to stem the Allied drive in the south. They had observed the regrouping of Allied troops and Allied naval preparations in the Naples area; and they believed that the Allies had sufficient strength both to maintain the offensive along the main fighting front and to attempt a landing in the Rome area. But they hoped to delay such an invasion by counterattacking in the south; then, after stopping the Allies on the Garigliano, they would draw back enough troops to check a landing.

## The Assault

In early January, VI Corps troops assembled in the Naples area to embark on a short but strenuous amphibious training program. Night operations and physical conditioning through speed marches were stressed. Infantry battalions practiced special beach assault tactics, landings under simulated

THE ANZIO LANDING *was virtually unopposed. These scenes, photographed at Yellow Beach soon after dawn on 22 January, show troops of the 3d Division (left) as they waded the last few yards to shore and (below) a line of vehicles moving inland. White tape indicates boundary of the path to which vehicles were confined by soft ground in the area.*

ENEMY COASTAL DEFENSES *were sparse and mostly unmanned.*
*These four photos, all taken in the Nettuno area, show the type of defenses the Germans had set up. The cannon is an obsolete model.*

fire, removing mine fields and barbed wire, and knocking out pillboxes on the beach. Artillerymen learned the knack of loading and unloading DUKW-borne 105-mm. howitzers. Assault landings were practiced and repracticed, first from mock-ups on dry land and then in battalion and regimental landing exercises with craft provided by the Navy. The program culminated in WEBFOOT, a Corps landing exercise lasting from 17 to 19 January on the beaches south of Salerno.[5]

As D Day approached, massed squadrons of medium and heavy bombers roared out toward

[5] During the WEBFOOT exercise the 3d Division lost one battalion of field artillery due to DUKW's swamping when put into the sea too far off shore during bad weather. This illustrates the absolute necessity for proper loading and trained crews in the use of this type of equipment. Very few men were drowned, but the DUKW's and all equipment went to the bottom. This battalion was replaced by a battalion of the 45th Division before the 3d Division sailed for Anzio.

northern Italy to strike the first blow in the new offensive. Their role was to choke off the vulnerable Italian rail and highway routes down which enemy supplies and reinforcements could flow toward the beachhead and the southern front. Shifting their weight from one main line to another, Fortresses, Liberators, Mitchells, Marauders, and Wellingtons hammered at key bridges and railroad yards from Rome north to the Brenner Pass. Closer to the front, fighters and light bombers strafed and bombed transport on the rail and highway nets. Finally, a few days before the landing, heavy bombers flew missions against key airfields in Italy and southern France to forestall any interference from the Luftwaffe with the Anzio assault.

While the Anzio landing was still in preparation, main Fifth Army began its southern drive. At dawn on 12 January, troops of the French Expeditionary Corps surged forward in the mountains above Cassino. While the French sought to turn the German left flank above Cassino, the British 10 Corps struck across the lower Garigliano to pierce the other flank of the Gustav Line. In spite of successive assaults neither the British nor the French were able to break through the rock-ribbed wall of German mountain defenses. In the center, on 20 January, the U.S. II Corps attacked in an effort to cross the Rapido and secure a bridgehead. After gaining a precarious foothold in two days of bitter fighting, heavy losses forced it to withdraw. By 22 January, D Day for the Anzio landing, the attack on the Gustav Line had bogged down in the midst of savage German counterattacks. Although Fifth Army had not succeeded in driving up the Liri Valley, the battle for Cassino continued and the Germans had been forced to commit most of *Tenth Army's* reserves. High hopes were still held that the Anzio landing would break the stalemate in the Liri Valley.

During the third week in January, Naples and its satellite ports were the scene of feverish activity as troops and supplies were loaded on a convoy of more than 250 ships and craft. Long lines of water-proofed vehicles rolled down to the docks and troops filed aboard the waiting ships. As dawn colored the hills above the Bay of Naples on 21 January, the first ships slipped their hawsers and the convoy sailed.

It had been impossible to conceal craft concentrations in the Naples area, but elaborate efforts were made to deceive the enemy as to the time and place of the assault, which might fall anywhere from Gaeta to Leghorn. The convoy plowed north from Naples at a steady 5-knot pace, swinging wide on a roundabout course to deceive the enemy as to its destination and to avoid mine fields. Allied air raids, however, had temporarily knocked out the German reconnaissance base at Perugia, and not an enemy plane was sighted in the sun-lit sky. Mine sweepers cleared a channel ahead, destroyers and cruisers clung to the flanks to ward

LT. GEN. MARK W. CLARK, *Commanding General of the Fifth Army, arriving at the beachhead on D Day morning in a Navy PT boat. He is shown reading radio dispatches on the battle's progress with a Fifth Army Staff officer.*

A DESTROYED MUSSOLINI CANAL BRIDGE *near Borgo Sabotino, part of the reconnaissance effort on the right flank on D Day. Photo, taken later, shows a treadway bridge over the canal, concrete road blocks (German) on the far side, and a trench system dug by American forces.*

off U-boats, and an air umbrella of fighters criss-crossed constantly. Actually, these elaborate precautions were hardly necessary, for the enemy air reconnaissance failed to observe either the embarkation at Naples or the approach of VI Corps to Anzio. Aboard the convoy men lolled about the decks, sleeping or sunbathing, checking equipment, or excitedly discussing what they would find. As night fell and darkness cloaked the convoy's movements, it swung sharply in toward Anzio.

At five minutes past midnight on 22 January, in the murky blackness off Cape Anzio, the assault convoy dropped anchor and rode easily on a calm Mediterranean Sea. There was a murmur of subdued activity as officers gave last-minute instructions, men clambered into stubby assault craft,

and davits swung out and lowered them to the sea. Patrol boats wove in and out of the milling craft herding them into formation, and then led the first waves away into the moonless night.

To gain surprise the guns of the escorting warships kept silent. Then, just ten minutes before H Hour (0200), a short, terrific rocket bombardment from two British LCT(R)'s burst with a deafening roar along the beach. These newly developed rocket craft, each carrying 798 5-inch rockets, were employed to disorganize any possible enemy ambush, explode mine fields along the beach, and destroy enemy beach defenses. But the attackers saw no burst of answering fire; when the rocket ships ceased firing, the shore again loomed dark and silent ahead.

As the first wave of craft hit the beach and men rushed for the cover of the dunes behind, there was no enemy to greet them. Pushing rapidly inland the astonished troops soon realized that the highly unexpected had happened. They had caught the enemy completely off guard. Although the Germans knew an amphibious landing was impending, they believed that it would not occur until somewhat later. The two divisions that had been assigned to guard this coast had been sent to the southern front only three days before, and the coastal sector and area south of Rome were held by only skeleton forces. Consequently, except for a few small coast artillery and antiaircraft detachments, the only immediate resistance to the Anzio landing came from scattered elements of the *29th Panzer Grenadier Division.* Only three engineer companies and the *2d Battalion, 71st Panzer Grenadier Regiment,* had been left to guard the coast from the mouth of the Tiber River through Anzio to the Mussolini Canal; one 9-mile stretch of the coast was occupied by a single company. Furthermore, the troops in the Anzio area had not been warned that an Allied landing was imminent. The coastal defenses were limited to scattered mine fields along Peter Beach used by the British 1 Division; some pillboxes, most of which were not even manned; and scattered artillery pieces—a few 88's and several old Italian,

French, and Yugoslav pieces—most of which were not even fired against the attackers.

Aided by a calm sea and the virtual absence of opposition, the invaders quickly established themselves on shore. (Map No. 3.) On the right, the 3d Division swept in over the beaches east of Nettuno. Brushing aside a few dazed enemy patrols, they pushed rapidly inland, established themselves on the initial phase line, and dug in to repel any counterattack. General Clark, accompanied by Brig. Gen. Donald W. Brann and other members of the Fifth Army Staff, arrived at the beachhead in a Navy PT boat, transferred to a DUKW, and landed at 1000. Motorized patrols of the 3d Reconnaissance and Provisional Reconnaissance Troops forged ahead to seize and blow the bridges over the Mussolini Canal which ran along the right flank. Only at the southernmost bridge did they meet any Germans. Here they knocked out three armored cars with bazookas,

ENGINEERS CLEARING DEMOLITION CHARGES IN ANZIO
*on D Day. The Germans failed to carry out their plans to destroy the port. Explosives, such as these men of the 36th Engineers are seen removing had been set so that buildings would topple into the streets, and thus hinder use of port facilities.*

AN AIR ATTACK ON CISTERNA *by medium bombers shows smoke and dust rising from bomb hits on enemy installations and the railroad just south of the town. Note the narrow, winding Cisterna Creek directly below plane.*

killing or capturing eleven of the enemy patrol.

The Ranger Force landed over the small beach just to the right of Anzio harbor and swiftly seized the port. The Rangers scrambled up the steep bluff, topped with pink and white villas overlooking the beach, and spread through the streets of the town, rounding up a few bewildered defenders. The Germans had had no time to demolish the port facilities. Except for a gap in the mole and some battered buildings along the waterfront (damage caused by Allied bombers), the only obstacles were a few small vessels sunk in the harbor. Later in the morning the 509th Parachute Infantry Battalion advanced east along the shore road and by 1015 occupied Nettuno. Northwest of Anzio the landing of the British 1 Division was equally un-opposed, although delayed by poor beach conditions. By noon of D Day VI Corps had reached all its preliminary objectives ashore.

In support of the landing, Allied fighter and bomber squadrons flew more than 1,200 sorties on D Day. Medium and heavy bombers blasted key bridges and such road junctions as Cisterna and Velletri in an attempt to block the main roads leading toward the Anzio area. Fighter-bombers, fighters, and night intruders ranged these highways, bombing and strafing the enemy traffic beginning to surge toward the beachhead. Other fighters gave continuous air cover to the landing force. Enemy air attacks were comparatively slight on D Day, totaling 140 sorties, but increased in intensity on 23 January.

PUTTING DOWN ROAD MATTING *at the beach exits was one of the problems confronting the engineers after the landings. Many heavy vehicles and the rapid supply build-up made the construction of a number of such roadways necessary.*

Behind the assault troops pushing inland, unloading of the initial convoy proceeded at a rapid pace. Engineers swiftly cleared the scattered mine fields and bulldozed exit roads across the dunes; but the clay soil between the beaches and the main road soon became so badly rutted that matting, corduroy, and rock had to be laid down to make the area passable. DUKW's and small craft scurried back and forth across the calm waters of Nettuno Bay, busily unloading the larger craft which were unable to approach the shallow beach. In spite of sporadic shelling after daylight from a few long-range German batteries inland and three small hit-and-run raids by Luftwaffe fighter-bombers, the 540th Engineers quickly moved streams of men and supplies across the beach. A mine sweeper hit a mine and one LCI was sunk by the bombs, but this was the only major damage. The 36th Engineers began clearing the debris from the port of Anzio; the Navy hauled away the sunken vessels. By early afternoon the port was ready to handle LST's and other craft. When the British beach northwest of Anzio proved to be too shallow for effective use, it was closed and British unloading switched to the newly opened port. By midnight of D Day some 36,000 men, 3,200 vehicles,

and large quantities of supplies were ashore, roughly 90 percent of the equipment and personnel of the assault convoy.

Casualties for D Day were light. Thirteen killed, ninety-seven wounded, and forty-four captured or missing were reported to VI Corps. Two hundred and twenty-seven prisoners were taken. Against negligible opposition VI Corps had reached its preliminary objectives and captured almost intact the port of Anzio, which was to be the key channel for supplies.

## Expanding the Beachhead

Having reached its preliminary objectives by noon of D Day, VI Corps moved forward to occupy the ground within the planned initial beachhead line. The British 1 Division advanced from its beaches on the left toward the Moletta River and gained control of seven miles of the Albano road. In the 3d Division sector the advance resolved itself into a series of actions to gain the bridges over the Mussolini Canal, vital to the defense of the right side of the beachhead.

By the evening of D Day, advance guards of the 30th Infantry and the 3d Reconnaissance Troop

UNLOADING AT ANZIO'S DOCKS *began D Day afternoon when the engineers cleared the harbor. LST's (left) were able to nose directly into the docks and soon afterward British troops (above) were moving through the battered port instead of over the shallow northern beaches.*

had seized all of the bridges across the canal. The enemy regained most of the bridges that night in attacks by aggressive, tank-supported attacks launched by elements of the *Hermann Goering Panzer Division.* The next morning Lt. Col. Lionel C. McGarr, commander of the 30th Infantry, brought up the remainder of his regiment, supported by tanks and tank destroyers; in sharp fighting it drove the enemy back across the bridges along the west branch. The Germans counterattacked with three tanks and a half-track to regain the bridge on the Cisterna road north of Conca, but the 30th Infantry's supporting armor drove them off. On the right of the 30th Infantry, the 504th Parachute Infantry, which had come ashore in Corps reserve, on 24 January relieved the 3d Reconnaissance Troop along the main canal and retook the other lost bridges.

By 24 January the 3d Division had occupied the right sector of the initial beachhead along the Mussolini Canal. The 504th Parachute Infantry held the right flank along the main canal; in the center the 15th Infantry, and on its left the 30th Infantry, faced Cisterna along the west branch. Ranger Force relieved all but the 3d Battalion, 7th Infantry, on the division left in the quiet central beachhead sector. Meanwhile the 2 Brigade of the 1 Division, under the command of Brig. E. E. J. Moore, rounded out its sector of the beachhead by advancing to the Moletta River line. The remainder of the division was held in Corps reserve in anticipation of an enemy counterattack. In two days VI Corps had secured a beachhead seven miles deep against only scattered opposition.

Although the Anzio landing and initial Allied build-up were virtually unopposed by German land forces, the enemy reacted swiftly to meet the emergency. Headquarters of *Army Group C* immediately alerted elements of the *4th Parachute* and *Hermann Goering Panzer Divisions* south of Rome and ordered them to defend the roads leading from Anzio toward Colli Laziali. At 0600 on 22 January it set in motion the prearranged plan to rush troops from outside of Italy to stem the Allied invasion. Two divisions and many lesser units started at once from France, Yugoslavia, and Germany itself. Three divisions of the *Fourteenth Army* in northern Italy were alerted and left for the Rome area on 22–23 January. To command the defense, *I Parachute Corps* reestablished its headquarters in the area below Rome at 1700 on 22 January. All available reserves from the southern front or on their way to it were rushed toward Anzio; these included the *3d Panzer Grenadier* and *71st Infantry Divisions*, and the bulk of the *Hermann Goering Panzer Division*. While these forces were assembling, the German Air Force bombed the beachhead area and its supporting naval craft in order to delay an Allied advance inland. For the first two days, the German defenders believed that

ADVANCING TOWARD THE MUSSOLINI CANAL, *elements of the 504th Parachute Infantry on D plus 2 moved in small groups and then only when protected by smoke screens. The canal is just beyond the smoke on the horizon, about 1,000 yards from the building in the foreground.*

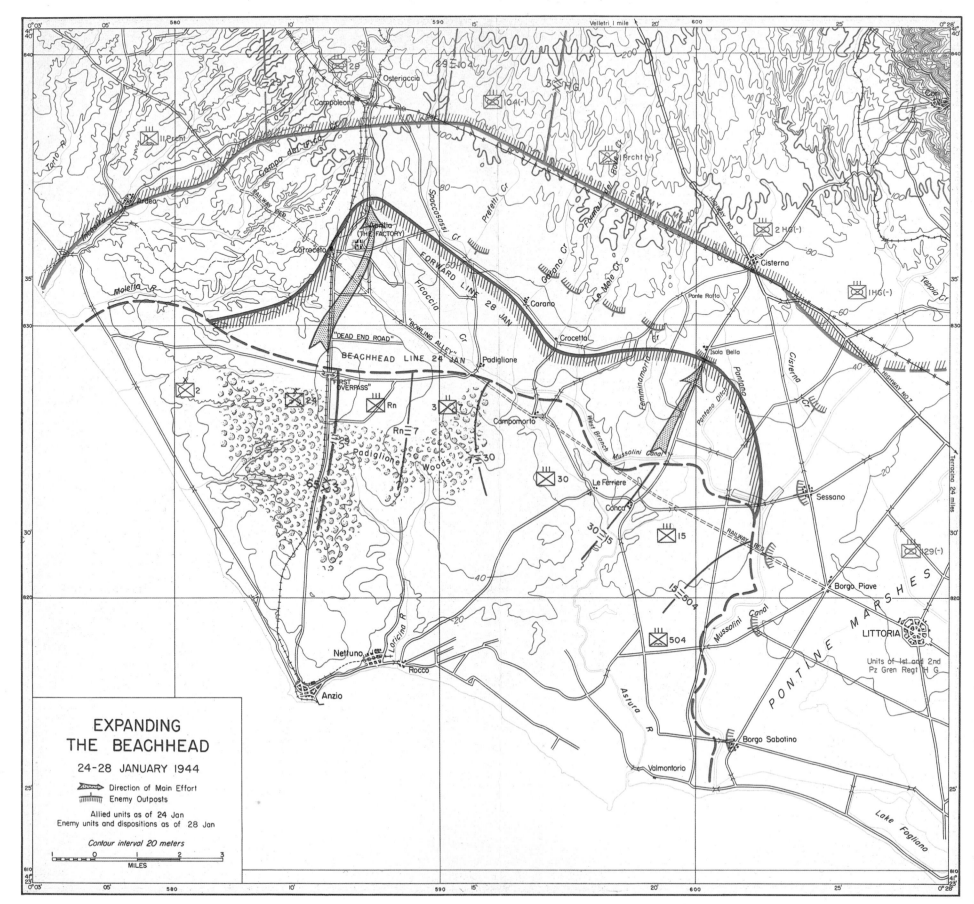

EXPANDING
THE BEACHHEAD

24-28 JANUARY 1944

Direction of Main Effort
Enemy Outposts

Allied units as of 24 Jan
Enemy units and dispositions as of 28 Jan

Contour interval 20 meters

1  0        1        2        3
MILES

MAP NO. 4

they were too weak to stop an Allied advance against Colli Laziali; but from the evening of 24 January they were confident that they could contain the beachhead forces and, as soon as they had substantially completed their concentration, launch a counterattack that would wipe out the Allied beachhead.

*Army Group C* on 24 January ordered the *Fourteenth Army* to take over the command of the German operations before Anzio. When the *Fourteenth Army*, commanded by Gen. Eberhard von Mackensen, assumed control on 25 January, elements of eight German divisions were employed in the defense line around the beachhead, and five more divisions with many supporting units were on their way to the Anzio area. By 28 January, *Fourteenth Army* had assigned command of the forces defending the eastern sector of the beachhead perimeter (before Cisterna) to the *Hermann Goering Panzer Division;* of the central sector (before Campoleone) to the *3d Panzer Grenadier Division;* and of the western sector (behind the Moletta River) to the *65th Infantry Division*. Behind this perimeter other units were grouped for counterattack. A gap of four or five miles separated the German main line of resistance from the main beachhead line occupied by the Allied VI Corps by 24 January.

The reaction of enemy forces gave no impetus to main Fifth Army's drive and made the prospect of linking the southern force with the beachhead remote. Also, if VI Corps extended itself too far inland toward Colli Laziali, its main objective, it would risk being cut off by a sudden German counterthrust. Before the end of D Day the Germans were estimated to have 20,000 troops in areas from which they could drive rapidly toward the beachhead. With the advantage of good communications, roads, and railroads, and in spite of Allied air interdiction, they had doubled that figure by D plus 2, and continued to increase it to more than 70,000 by D plus 7. This growing strength indicated that VI Corps would have to prepare to meet an enemy thrust calculated to drive the Allied forces back into the sea.

VI Corps consequently consolidated its positions during the period 24–29 January. While awaiting reinforcements, Allied troops probed along the two main axes of advance toward the intermediate objectives of Cisterna and Campoleone, which would serve as strategic jump-off points for the advance on Colli Laziali. On the right the 3d Division moved up the roads leading across the Mussolini Canal toward Cisterna; on the left the British pushed up the Albano road toward Campoleone.[6] (Map No. 4.)

On the afternoon of 24 January, four companies of the 15th and 30th Infantry made a preliminary reconnaissance in force toward Cisterna, but they were unable to make much headway against strong enemy mobile elements. General Truscott then ordered an advance in greater force at dawn on 25 January up the two main roads leading across the muddy fields toward the town. The 1st Battalion, 30th Infantry, advanced up the left-hand or Campomorto–Cisterna road, while the 2d Battalion, 15th Infantry, took the right up the Conca–Cisterna road.

About two miles beyond the canal the 30th Infantry was halted by a company of the *Hermann Goering Panzer Division,* intrenched around the road junction halfway to Ponte Rotto. On the right of the 30th Infantry, the 2d Battalion, 15th Infantry, gained one and one-half miles up the Conca–Cisterna road before it was stopped by German machine gunners concealed within the farmhouses along the route. Tanks and tank destroyers of the 751st Tank Battalion and the 601st Tank Destroyer Battalion were brought up to reduce these strong points. Before the armor could go into action German units infiltrated down a stream bed forcing the outposts along the 2d Battalion's right flank to withdraw. Company C, which was making a diversionary attack up a parallel road to the right of the Conca–Cisterna road, bogged down before similar resistance and four of its accompanying tanks were lost to an enemy self-

---

[6] Campoleone Station. The town of Campoleone is about a mile and a quarter north. References to Campoleone throughout this study are to the railroad station, not to the town proper.

propelled gun. With unexpected strength the veteran *Hermann Goering Panzer Division* had blunted the spearheads of the 3d Division attack. Not having time to prepare fixed defenses, the Germans had emplaced machine guns and anti-tank guns in every farmhouse along the roads. These strong points had excellent interlocking fields of fire across the gently rolling fields and were supported by roving tanks and self-propelled guns. They had to be knocked out one by one by American tanks and tank destroyers before the infantry could advance.

To assist the main effort, paratroopers of the 504th Parachute Infantry made a diversionary attack across the main canal toward Littoria. Advancing behind a heavy curtain of supporting fires, augmented by the guns of the cruiser *Brooklyn* and two destroyers, they captured the villages of Borgo Sabotino, Borgo Piave, and Sessano on the east side of the canal. Company D, however; was cut off beyond Borgo Piave by a surprise counter-thrust of five tanks and eight *flakwagons* (self-propelled antiaircraft guns) of the *Hermann Goer-*

*ing Panzer Division.* Company D lost heavily, though many of the men managed to infiltrate back. That night the 504th Parachute Infantry, leaving behind strong combat patrols, withdrew from its exposed positions.

The 3d Division resumed its push toward Cisterna the next morning, 26 January. In the 30th Infantry zone the 1st Battalion infiltrated around the road junction below Ponto Rotto where it had been held up, and forced the enemy to withdraw. That afternoon the 1st Battalion, 15th Infantry thrust northeast up the right-hand road across the west branch of the canal to establish a road block on the Cisterna–Littoria road. In spite of seventy minutes of massed supporting fire from the 9th, 10th, and 39th Field Artillery Battalions, and neutralizing fire by heavier guns, the Germans clung tenaciously to their positions. Behind a similar elaborate artillery preparation, the 2d Battalion, 15th Infantry, on 27 January pushed up the Conca–Cisterna road. At the same time the 1st Battalion, 15th Infantry, continued its attack on the right. It gained some ground but was unable to break

THE RIGHT FLANK AT THE MUSSOLINI CANAL *was covered by the 504th Parachute Infantry, dug in on the east bank. This position was west of Littoria, toward which a diversionary attack was launched in support of the 3d Division on 25 January.*

ENEMY SHELLFIRE HITTING THE BEACHES *did not halt the work of DUKW's which carried supplies from Liberty ships offshore. This sporadic shelling was considered a nuisance, but caused only limited damage.*

through to its objective. Rushing new units into the line piecemeal as fast as they arrived, the Germans were making every effort to keep the Americans from reaching Highway No. 7. In the attacks of 25–27 January the 3d Division reached positions one to two miles beyond the west branch of the Mussolini Canal; it was still three miles from Cisterna. It became evident that an effort greater than was immediately possible would be necessary to reach the division's objective. General Truscott therefore called a halt in the advance to regroup for a more concentrated drive.

To parallel the drive of the 3d Division, the British 1 Division had been ordered to move up the Albano road to Campoleone, to secure this im-

portant road and railway junction as a jump-off point for a further advance. With the arrival of the 179th Regimental Combat Team (45th Division), VI Corps released from Corps reserve the 24 Guards Brigade for this move. A strong mobile patrol up the road on 24 January surprised an enemy outpost at Carroceto and continued four miles farther inland to a point north of Campoleone. To exploit this apparent enemy weakness, General Penney on 25 January dispatched the 24 Guards Brigade, with one squadron of the 46 Royal Tanks and one medium and two field regiments of artillery in support, to take the Factory (Aprilia) near Carroceto. The *3d Battalion, 29th Panzer Grenadier Regiment (3d Panzer Grenadier Division),* however, had occupied the Factory the night before. The 1 Scots Guards and 1 Irish Guards pushed through a hasty mine field across the road, and the 5 Grenadier Guards then drove the enemy from the Factory, capturing 111 prisoners. (Map No. 4)

The enemy, sensitive to the loss of this strong point, counterattacked strongly the next morning. Twenty tanks and a battalion of the *29th Panzer Grenadier Regiment* thrust at the 5 Grenadier Guards in the Factory. Their main assault was repulsed, but they continued to feel around the flanks until they were finally driven off that afternoon. The Germans left behind four burning tanks, one self-propelled gun, and forty-six more prisoners. By the morning of 28 January the 24 Guards Brigade had advanced one and one-half miles north of the Factory. The 1 Division then paused to regroup for an attack on Campoleone.

By 29 January, VI Corps had expanded its beachhead by the advances of the 1 and 3d Division, but was still from two to four miles short of its two intermediate objectives. It was clear that an attack in greater strength would be necessary to continue the drive. The Corps paused to regroup. (Map No. 5.)

Behind the assault troops pushing inland, engineers and service troops worked day and night to organize the beachhead and prepare a firm base for the main attack. Roads were repaired, dumps established, and a beginning made on defenses to meet any future German counterthrusts. The port, vital to the supply build-up and troop reinforcement, was placed in such effective operation that by 1 February it could handle 8 LST's, 8 LCT's, and 5 LCI's simultaneously. Liberty ships, however, were unable to enter the shallow harbor and continued to be unloaded by DUKW's and LCT's over X-Ray and Yellow Beaches. The weather during the first week at Anzio turned out much better than anticipated and greatly facilitated the stockage of supplies. The port was usable in all but the worst weather, and only on two days during the first week, 24 and 26 January, was unloading over the beaches halted by high winds and surf. A gale during the night of 26 January blew ashore all ponton

causeways and beached 12 LCT's, 1 LST, and 1 LCI. In spite of these interruptions and enemy interference, 201 LST's and 7 Liberty ships had been completely unloaded by 31 January. On the peak day of 29 January 6,350 tons were unloaded: 3,155 tons through the port, 1,935 over X-Ray Beach, and 1,260 over Yellow Beach.

The beach and port areas, still within range of German artillery, were vulnerable targets for increasing shelling. Long-range 88-mm. and 170-mm. batteries dropped their shells sporadically on ships off shore and among troops working along the beach. Although this fire was a nuisance to the troops and interfered with work, it caused only limited damage in the early days. Floating mines continued to be a menace, damaging a destroyer and a mine sweeper. On 24 January an LST carrying Companies C and D, 83d Chemical Battalion, struck a mine. Most of the men were transferred to an LCI alongside, which also hit a mine and sank. Total casualties were 5 officers and 289 men.

Far more dangerous to beach and shipping were the constant Luftwaffe raids. The German Air Force put up its biggest air effort since Sicily in an attempt to cut off Allied supplies. Small flights of fighter-bombers strafed and bombed the beach and port areas every few hours. The most serious threat, however, was the raiding by medium bomber squadrons hastily brought back from Greece and the torpedo and glider bombers from airfields in southern France. Skimming in low at dusk from the sea through the smoke and hail of ack-ack fire, they released bombs, torpedoes, and radio-controlled glider bombs on the crowded shipping in the harbor. In three major raids, on 23, 24, and 26 January, they sank a British destroyer and a hospital ship, damaged another hospital ship, and beached a Liberty ship. The two heaviest raids came at dusk and midnight on 29 January, when 110 Dornier 217's, Junkers 88's, and Messerschmitt 210's sank a Liberty ship and the British antiaircraft cruiser *Spartan*.

Stiffening air defenses took a heavy toll of the Luftwaffe raiders, downing ninety-seven of them before 1 February. Initially Col. Edgar W. King

ANTIAIRCRAFT GUNS AND BARRAGE BALLOONS *appeared in increasing numbers as the German air raiders stepped up their attacks. The crew above mans a 40-mm. Bofors gun. Shown below is one of the low-level type balloons designed to counter strafing attacks.*

of the 68th Coast Artillery Regiment (Antiaircraft) and later Brig. Gen. Aaron A. Bradshaw, Jr., supervised the installation of increasing numbers of 40-mm. and 90-mm. antiaircraft guns and established a 12,000-yard inner artillery zone around the vital beach and port areas. Barrage balloons were raised to halt low-level bombing and smoke screens blanketed the port at dusk and on every red alert. The enemy's favorite tactic was to sneak over at dusk, when Allied planes, which needed daylight to take off, were returning to their 100-mile distant bases. To combat these sneak raids the engineers renovated the old Italian artillery school air strip at Nettuno. P–40's of the 307th Fighter Squadron moved up to the beachhead to furnish "on the spot" cover, and the Air Force increased its use of Beaufighter night patrols and Spitfires trained for night fighting.

Good weather during most of the first week at Anzio and the aid rendered by use of the port enabled the assault convoy to be unloaded rapidly and turned around to bring up the follow-up force. The 45th Division and the 1st Armored Division (less Combat Command B, which was retained for possible employment at Cassino) had reached the beachhead by 1 February. Essential Corps artillery, engineers, and signal troops had also arrived.

Although the Germans in the Anzio area outnumbered VI Corps by 30 January, it was believed that their defenses had not progressed beyond road blocks, hasty field fortifications, and mine fields along likely avenues of approach. Allied patrols could still operate freely to Highway No. 7 and Campoleone. The positions the enemy was constructing along the railroad between Campoleone and Cisterna were believed to be intended for delaying action. It was anticipated that his main stand against an Allied advance would more likely be along the high ground around Cori and Velletri.

In view of the rapidly increasing enemy build-up, General Lucas decided to launch his drive toward Colli Laziali before his forces might be too far

outnumbered. On 30 January the enemy forces in the beachhead area were estimated to number 71,500; VI Corps had 61,332 troops ashore on the same date. It was planned to resume the 3d Division push on Cisterna on 29 January, but the attack was delayed one day to permit the 1 Division and the 1st Armored Division to complete preparations for a coordinated offensive. On 30 January all three divisions were to attack.

The drive of VI Corps out of the Anzio beachhead was designed to coincide with a renewed offensive on the southern front. On main Fifth Army's front, II Corps was preparing to open its drive on Cassino on 1 February, with the 34th Division carrying the attack. The 10 Corps in the Garigliano sector continued the consolidation of the bridgehead which it had successfully established in an attack on 17–20 January. On the Eighth Army front the Canadian 1 Division was to attack in the coastal sector on 30 January.

The Germans originally planned to counterattack the Allied beachhead in force on 28 January. But Allied bombings of roads and railways, and a desire to await the arrival of reinforcements from Germany, led to a decision on 26 January to postpone the attack until 1 February. In preparation, the enemy proceeded to arrange his infantry and artillery into three combat groups. The principal assault was to be launched southward along the Albano–Anzio road (with the main concentration on either side of the Factory) by *Combat Group Graeser,* which would consist of seventeen infantry battalions heavily supported by artillery. While the main effort was to be made in the center, the Germans planned to launch simultaneous attacks all along the front on the morning of D Day, 1 February; these were to be preceded by a coordinated 10-minute artillery barrage. While the necessary regroupings were under way, Allied VI Corps launched its offensive on 30 January forcing the Germans to postpone their attack until after the Allied drive had been stopped.

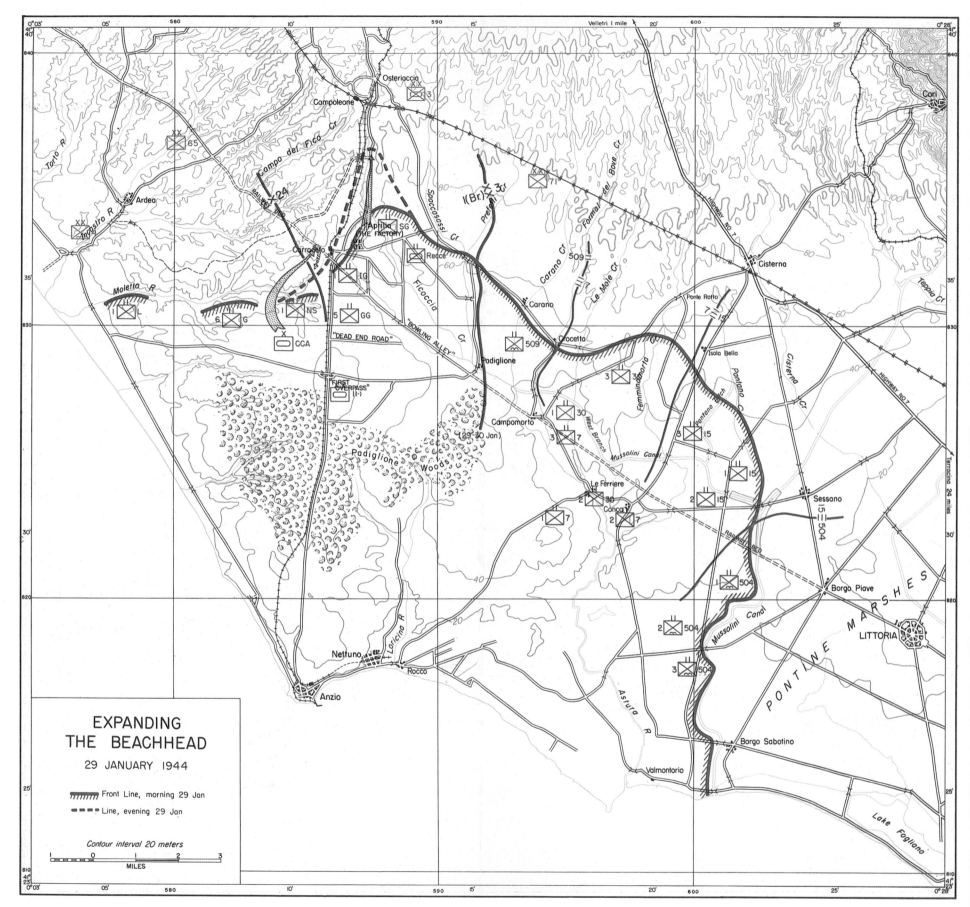

EXPANDING
THE BEACHHEAD

29 JANUARY 1944

Front Line, morning 29 Jan

Line, evening 29 Jan

Contour interval 20 meters

MILES

MAP NO. 5

# THE ALLIED OFFENSIVE
## (30 January–1 February)

The VI Corps plan for the attack in the direction of Colli Laziali on 30 January called for a two-pronged advance, with the main blow to be delivered on the left. On the right the 3d Division, reinforced by the 504th Parachute Infantry Regiment and Ranger Force, was to attack at dawn to cut Highway No. 7 at Cisterna. The capture of this key road junction would dislocate the German left flank and pave the way for a 3d Division thrust up Highway No. 7 to assault Colli Laziali from the east. On the left, the British 1 Division and the 1st Armored Division were to follow the Albano road axis, the best and most direct route inland. The 1 Division was to drive up the road toward the high ground above Albano and Genzano on the southwest slope of Colli Laziali, while the 1st Armored Division swung wide around the left of the 1 Division to come in on Colli Laziali from the west. (Map No. 21.) A preliminary artillery preparation was not considered necessary, but extensive supporting fires, a smoke screen laid by air at daylight, and naval gunfire support were planned. The air force prepared an elaborate air program, including special air cover for the advance of armor. Once VI Corps attained the commanding heights of Colli Laziali, it would be astride vital enemy communications routes and so threaten to cut off the German forces in the south. The need for careful control and coordination of the advance was recognized by General Lucas, for the missions of the right and of the left were initially divergent in direction; should

VI Corps be overextended, the enemy might take the opportunity of splitting the Allied forces.

In order to concentrate on a narrower front for the offensive, the 1 and 3d Divisions regrouped on 28–29 January. These divisions were relieved along the beachhead flanks by the 45th Division so that they could employ their full strength in the advance. Elements of the 45th Division and Corps engineers took over the positions of the 2 Brigade along the Moletta River and of the 504th Parachute Infantry on the opposite flank along the Mussolini Canal. At the same time Ranger Force and the 3d Battalion, 7th Infantry, were relieved by the 1 Reconnaissance Regiment in the quiet central beachhead sector.

As VI Corps prepared to launch its offensive toward Cisterna and Campoleone on 30 January, the German forces were being regrouped for a major counteroffensive. Thirty infantry battalions, supported by armor and artillery, were being organized into combat groups for this offensive, and six more infantry battalions were to be held in reserve. The German main line of resistance was established in front of Cisterna and Campoleone, and forward positions were strongly held. *Fourteenth Army* was completing its preparations for the execution of its main mission, the annihilation of the beachhead.

A message from Berlin to *Fourteenth Army* on 28 January reported that, according to reliable sources, the Allies were planning a second landing at Civitavecchia, north of the Tiber. The Germans drew some troops from the Anzio area to meet this threat, and on 31 January ordered a thorough demolition of the harbor installations at Civitavecchia. On 2 February, headquarters of *Army Group C* declared that such an invasion was probable; some additional forces were diverted to the Civitavecchia area. The effect of these diversions was to weaken somewhat the German defense forces around Anzio.

## Attack on Cisterna, 30 January

On 30 January the 3d Division launched its drive to cut Highway No. 7 at Cisterna. (Map No. 6.) To spearhead the attack, General Truscott picked Col. William O. Darby's Rangers, veterans of Tunisia, Sicily, and Salerno. The 1st and 3d Ranger Battalions were to jump off one hour before the main attack and infiltrate under cover of darkness four miles across the fields to seize Cisterna by surprise and hold it until the main attack came up. The 4th Rangers and the 3d Battalion, 15th Infantry, were to follow an hour later up the Conca–Cisterna road. Patrol reports and a careful reconnaissance of approach routes indicated that the enemy had not yet been able to consolidate his defenses in front of Cisterna; Colonel Darby believed his men could sift through. Then at H Hour, 0200, the 7th and 15th Infantry would launch the main attack. On the left, the 7th Infantry was to pass through the 30th Infantry and drive northeast to get astride Highway No. 7 above Cisterna, while the 15th Infantry would thrust north behind the Rangers to cut Highway No. 7 below the town. At the same time the 504th Parachute Infantry was to make a diversionary attack along the Mussolini Canal to protect the division's right flank.

Men of the 1st and 3d Rangers, each with two bandoleers of ammunition slung over his shoulders and with pockets stuffed with grenades, slipped across the west branch of the Mussolini Canal at 0130 on their mission to Cisterna. In column of battalions they crept silently forward along the narrow Pantano ditch, which runs northwest across the fields to the right of the Conca–Cisterna road. Concealed beneath a moonless cloudy sky, the long snake-like column moved past numerous German positions which they could see and hear on all sides. Several times Rangers hugged the sides of the ditch as German sentries walked by on its bank. By dawn the head of the leading battalion had come out of the ditch where it crossed the road and was within 800 yards of Cisterna. The 3d followed directly behind, the tail of the column just clearing the road running east from Isola Bella.

When dawn revealed the head of the column moving down the road to Cisterna, a strong German force led by three self-propelled guns suddenly opened fire. The Rangers deployed quickly and knocked out the three guns. But as the light improved, German machine guns, mortars, and snipers, concealed in houses and haystacks or dug in all around them, trapped the Rangers in a hail of fire. Caught without cover in the open treeless fields, and with their chance for surprise completely lost, the Rangers scrambled for the ditches and houses, firing back at a hidden enemy. The Germans, anticipating a renewal of the attack on Cisterna, had brought in veteran troops the night before to stiffen the defense. Evidently the enemy had also detected the Rangers' approach through their lines and had had time to prepare an ambush.

The Rangers fought desperately all through the morning against intrenched Germans all about them. At 0730 the 1st Battalion broke radio silence to report the situation in its struggle to get a foothold in Cisterna. An hour later a handful of Rangers had inched forward to take a few buildings near the railroad station at the edge of the town, but most of the men were still pinned down in the open fields.

The 4th Rangers and 3d Battalion, 15th Infantry, jumping off an hour later than the 1st and 3d Rangers, made every effort to respond to their appeals for help. The 4th Rangers advanced up the Conca–Cisterna road but were stopped by heavy enemy machine-gun fire from a group of farm houses below Isola Bella. Lt. Col. Roy A. Murray, battalion commander, sought to outflank this island

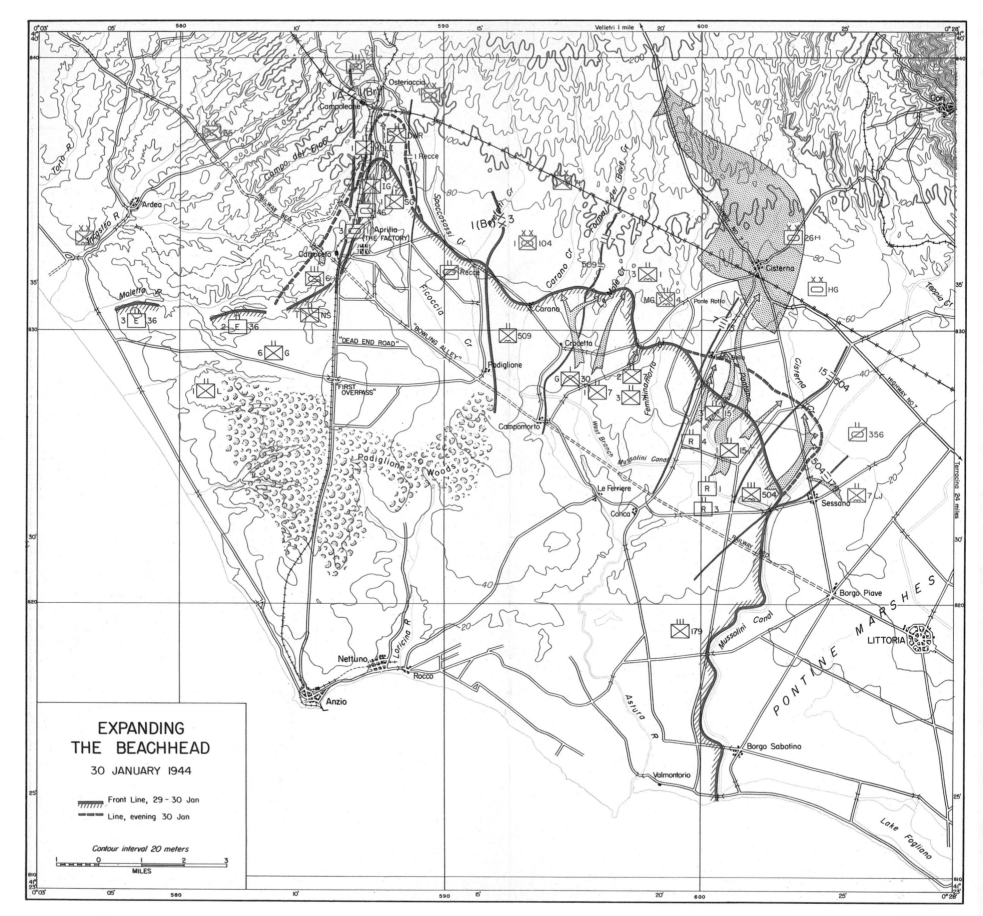

EXPANDING
THE BEACHHEAD

30 JANUARY 1944

Front Line, 29 - 30 Jan

Line, evening 30 Jan

Contour interval 20 meters

MILES

MAP NO. 6

of resistance and pushed to within a mile of Isola Bella before dawn broke. As soon as the Germans could locate the attackers accurately, they kept the battalion under well-aimed fire in the open fields. Stopped in their first effort to relieve the trapped battalions, the 4th Rangers attempted a breakthrough with two tank destroyers and two half-tracks, but two of the vehicles ran afoul of a mine field below Isola Bella. A second attempt also failed. All day the Germans held the 4th Rangers, who suffered heavy casualties in exchanging fire with an enemy only 200 yards away.

Meanwhile along the road below Cisterna the 1st and 3d Rangers were almost at the end of their strength. About noon enemy tanks came down from Highway No. 7 and raced back and forth through the Ranger positions. Firing up and down the ditches, they forced the Rangers into the open

ISOLA BELLA AND CISTERNA, *the focal points of the right flank attack to cut Highway No. 7, were connected by the Conca-Cisterna road across flat, open ground. The 1st and 3d Rangers advanced up Pantano ditch; the 4th Rangers attacked toward Isola Bella (foreground) to clear the way for the 15th Infantry.*

and split them into small groups. Lacking antitank guns or heavy weapons, the Rangers fought back with bazookas and sticky grenades. One enemy tank was quickly set aflame. As a second tank rumbled down on a squad commanded by Sgt. Thomas B. Fergen, he hit it with a sticky grenade. One of his men blasted it with a bazooka and another finished the tank off by climbing up on it and dropping a grenade down the turret.

As the tanks closed in, the shattered companies attempted to withdraw. It was too late. The Germans had surrounded them and they were unable to break through. As a last resort the few remaining officers ordered the troops to scatter through the fields and escape. At 1230, 1st Sgt. Robert E. Ehalt of the 3d Battalion sent a final message from the battalion command post. Only ten men were left around him, he was out of contact with all the companies, and he was destroying his radio as the tanks approached. Of 767 men in the Ranger attack only six escaped. Most of the men were captured by the Germans.

A platoon of forty-three men of the 3d Reconnaissance Troop, which had followed the road behind the Rangers to outpost their line, also was trapped. The men tried to escape down the road in their jeeps but piled up on a German road block. Only one man got back.

The American troops that advanced toward Cisterna on the morning of 30 January ran into a heavy concentration of German forces—elements of the *Hermann Goering Panzer Division* and supporting units—instead of the thinly held outpost positions which they expected. The German main line of resistance was in front of Cisterna, not behind it. Thus the Germans were able to destroy or capture the advanced elements that approached Cisterna, and to slow the American drive all along the front.

When the 4th Rangers were stopped along the road below Isola Bella, the 3d Battalion, 15th Infantry, which was to push up behind them, was unable to launch its planned attack. On General Truscott's order, Lt. Col. Ashton H. Manhart, commander of the 15th Infantry, directed the 3d Battalion to swing off the road to the east and follow

the route of the 1st and 3d Rangers, in an effort to reinforce them. After the Rangers surrendered, this battalion was ordered to turn toward Isola Bella and attack it from the right rear. Under cover of a heavy concentration of smoke and shells laid down on the village, the battalion found a gap in the enemy defenses and filtered across the soggy fields. Behind their tanks and tank destroyers they drove in on the battered, rubble-filled cluster of buildings, firing at point-blank range to clear each house of its defenders. By noon they had overcome all organized resistance, although they were kept busy all afternoon hunting down snipers and small groups of Germans who infiltrated through the lines. Too late to save the 1st and 3d Rangers, Maj. Frederick W. Boye, Jr., swung his 3d Battalion south from Isola Bella to clear out enemy pockets holding up the 4th Rangers along the road.

Meanwhile, the 1st Battalion, 15th Infantry, drove up the parallel road about two miles to the right of the 3d Battalion to clear the regiment's right flank. Against strong opposition the battalion pushed forward a mile and a half to reach its objective. Tanks of Company B, 751st Tank Battalion, spearheading the infantry's advance, knocked out a Mark IV tank, overran three 75-mm. antitank guns, and rounded up remnants of two shattered companies of the *Hermann Goering Panzer Division*.

In a diversionary attack on the 3d Division's right flank, the 504th Parachute Infantry thrust north along the main Mussolini Canal. The paratroopers' mission was to seize and blow two bridges north of the canal junction and to cut Highway No. 7 in order to block these possible avenues of counterattack. After a stiff fight the 1st Battalion reached both bridges, but before it could seize them, the Germans blew them up. While the 1st Battalion mopped up the Germans on the near side of the canal, capturing large numbers of prisoners from the *Hermann Goering Panzer Division* and the *356th Reconnaissance Battalion,* the 2d Battalion, under Lt. Col. Daniel W. Danielson, attacked through the 1st Battalion toward Highway No. 7. Their advance was held up, however, along

EACH BUILDING BECAME A FORTRESS *as the opposing forces battled for protection and cover afforded by scattered farmhouses on the featureless right-flank terrain. Here a German artillery shell bursts on a building near Cisterna occupied by American troops.*

the ravine formed by Cisterna Creek, because the Germans had blown the bridges, making it impossible to put supporting armor across the stream gully. In the afternoon, the newly arrived *7th Luftwaffe Jaeger Battalion* attacked across the main canal, striking the paratroopers in the rear. This enemy shock battalion was made up of hardened disciplinary offenders of the German Air Force who had chosen combat service and a clean slate to military prison. The thrust was stopped by the 69th Armored Field Artillery Battalion in a hot hour of rapid firing.

Forming the left prong of the 3d Division attack, the 7th Infantry, under the command of Col. Harry B. Sherman, was to cut Highway No. 7 above Cisterna. The 1st Battalion made a long night march to the line of departure and then at 0200, 30 January, launched its attack north along Le Mole Creek to cut the highway before daylight; the 2d Battalion's attack up the Crocetta–Cisterna road did not get started until 1115. The day before the attack the 30th Infantry had still been fighting for the area designated as the 1st Battalion's line of

departure. Consequently, Lt. Col. Frank M. Izenour, the 1st Battalion commander, had been unable to make a detailed reconnaissance of the route of advance and was forced to rely mainly on air photographs. Before the 1st Battalion had advanced very far, the troops found that what had appeared to be evenly spaced hedgerows in the aerial photographs were actually 20-foot drainage ditches overgrown with briars. These barriers greatly hampered the night movement and the tanks, which were unable to cross them in the dark, had to be left behind. The infantry had pressed forward a mile and a half across the fields on both sides of the creek when suddenly a burst of German flares starkly outlined the troops against the dark ground. All around them the enemy opened fire. Daylight revealed the battalion caught in a small pocket formed by low knolls to the front, left, and right rear. From his positions on the three knolls the enemy poured down automatic fire. The men dived for cover of the ditches, but each ditch seemed enfiladed by German machine guns. The battalion suffered heavy losses; Colonel Izenour and about 150 others, men

TANKS TAKE MOMENTARY COVER *behind a farm building while smoke is put down to cover their advance. These tanks were part of the armor accompanying the 7th and 15th Infantry in the attack on 31 January which carried them to within a mile of Cisterna.*

and officers, were hit. Capt. William P. Athas of the heavy weapons company hastily set up four machine guns, and under their protecting fire the riflemen deployed and drove the Germans from the hill to the right rear. During the day, 246 men of the scattered battalion filtered through to rally on this knoll. Maj. Frank Sinsel was sent forward to take command of the battalion and, after daylight, tanks managed to negotiate the ditches and came up in support. All day the 1st Battalion, too weak to attack, held its ground under the battering of enemy artillery and mortar fire. Reinforcements were sent up through the ditches that night, but the enemy, with guns sited accurately on the ditches, subjected the troops moving up to heavy shell fire.

The 2d Battalion attack up the road toward Cisterna was also delayed. Its tanks were unable to move up through the smoke and artillery fire laid down by supporting units. When the troops finally crossed the line of departure they were thrown back almost immediately by a unit of the *1st Parachute Division,* which had moved in the night before and dug in around the road junction south of Ponte

Rotto. To renew the attack that afternoon, Colonel Sherman added his reserve 3d Battalion. He ordered Maj. William B. Rosson, the battalion commander, to clean up the road junction from the south and go on to the high ground overlooking Ponte Rotto. The Sherman tanks and M–10 tank destroyers operating with the battalion rumbled up over the gravel road, systematically demolishing each German-held farmhouse and haystack barring the way. Behind the screen of armor and intensive artillery and mortar concentrations, the infantry cleared the road junction from the south and pushed on to seize their objective, the knoll above Ponte Rotto, by daylight on 31 January. In the first day's assault the 7th Infantry had gained about half the distance to Cisterna.

In view of the unexpectedly strong German resistance against the 3d Division and the failure of the Ranger infiltration, General Truscott ordered his division to reorganize along the Ponte Rotto–Isola Bella–Cisterna Creek phase line before resuming the attack. Instead of the incomplete defenses and limited forces it had expected to find

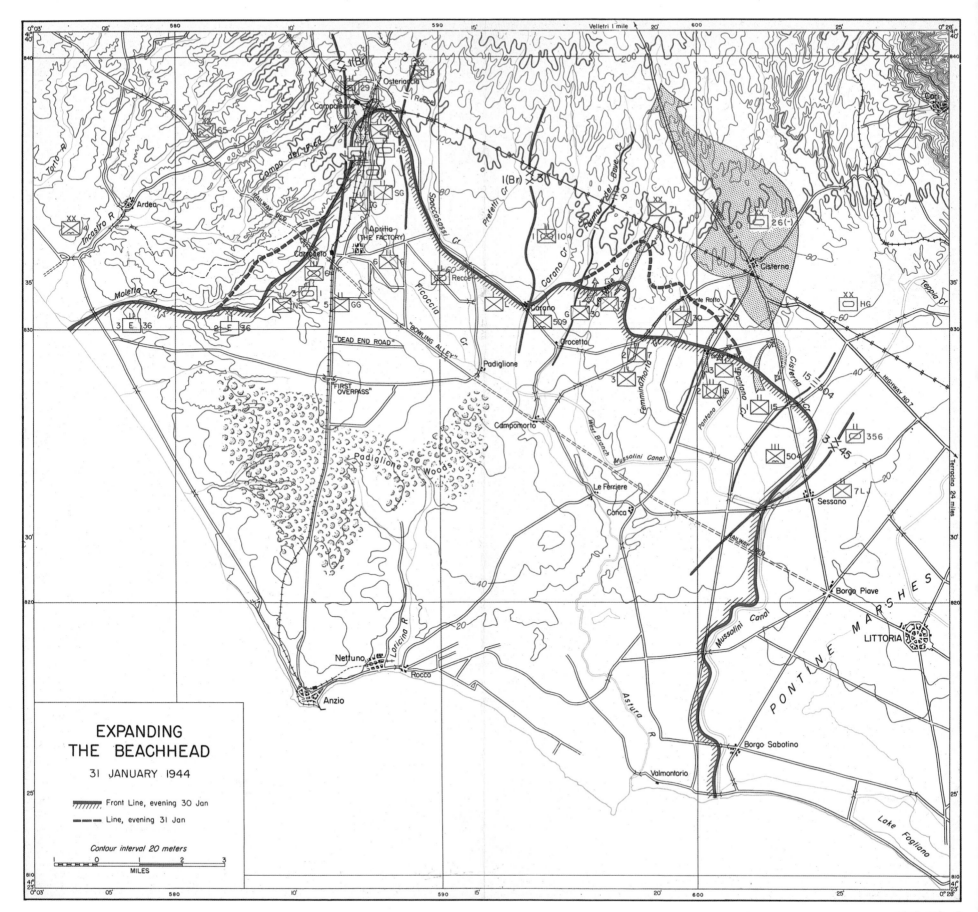

EXPANDING
THE BEACHHEAD

31 JANUARY 1944

Front Line, evening 30 Jan

Line, evening 31 Jan

Contour interval 20 meters

MILES

MAP NO. 7

before Cisterna, the 3d Division had run into strongly manned and well-prepared positions. Anticipating a renewal of the drive on Highway No. 7, the enemy moved in fresh troops to reinforce the depleted *Hermann Goering Panzer Division.* Against such resistance the 7th and 15th Infantry had gained over a mile and a half in the first day's attack but were still almost two miles from their goal. During the afternoon and evening of 30 January the 3d Division cleaned up remaining pockets of German resistance behind the forward line, brought up reinforcements and ammunition, and prepared to renew the drive toward Cisterna the next day.

## Attack on Cisterna, 31 January–1 February

With less than two miles separating them from their goal, the 7th and 15th Infantry resumed their attack on the afternoon of 31 January. (Map No. 7.) Instead of driving toward Highway No. 7 north and south of Cisterna they were to advance up the Ponte Rotto and Isola Bella roads to converge on the town itself. This time General Truscott employed the full weight of all his supporting weapons to beat down the German defenses which had held up the previous day's attack. The infantry advance was preceded by successive artillery concentrations. Division and attached artillery fired 1,216 missions (630 of them observed) during 31 January. The Air Force laid a smoke screen behind Cisterna at daylight to conceal the attack, and the 84th Chemical Battalion put down screening white phosphorus fire. Assault guns, tanks, and tank destroyers accompanied the infantry. Although extremely heavy air cooperation was planned, including an attack on Cisterna at H Hour by 70 B–26's, most of the program was canceled because of low clouds.

Prior to the attack, on the morning of 31 January, the 4th Rangers cleared out the remaining pockets of German resistance on the road below Isola Bella. They crept forward through the muddy ditches and, aided by two tanks and two assault guns, stormed the last houses blocking the road. By noon the Rangers had forced their way through

to link up with the 15th Infantry, which had taken Isola Bella the previous day. In the afternoon, light tanks of Company D, 751st Tank Battalion, assisted the Rangers in rounding up 150 Germans cut off and left isolated in the fields on both sides of the road.

On the division right, the 15th Infantry, its line of communication now cleared behind it, attacked on the afternoon of 31 January from Isola Bella. The fresh 2d Battalion passed through the 3d and drove northeast up the Cisterna road. The advance was preceded by massed fires of the 39th and 69th Field Artillery Battalions and the 1st Battalion, 77th Field Artillery Regiment. Knocking out three German tanks and an assault gun, the troops fought their way across the fields toward the white buildings less than two miles away. German resistance was solid. The German defenders clung stubbornly to their intrenched positions before Cisterna. By nightfall the 2d Battalion had gained a mile of the remaining distance to Cisterna, but it was still only half way to its goal.

Behind the 2d Battalion the other two battalions of the 15th Infantry cleaned out the German pockets in the fields between Isola Bella and the Cisterna–Littoria road. The 3d Battalion, advancing east along the lateral road from Isola Bella, was strongly counterattacked by seven German tanks driving across the fields from Cisterna. The situation became critical. Three of the four accompanying tank destroyers of Company B, 601st Tank Destroyer Battalion, had been disabled previously, but Sgt. W. E. Nesmith's M–10, last one of the platoon, halted the threatened enemy breakthrough with well-aimed fire. During the fight he drilled one enemy tank with three shots and the others withdrew. Meanwhile, on the right of the 3d Battalion, the 1st Battalion continued its push northeast to reach the Cisterna–Littoria road. The Germans reacted swiftly. Infantry supported by tanks struck the 1st Battalion in the right flank, knocked out two supporting tank destroyers and a tank, and forced the battalion back 1,000 yards. At the close of 31 January, the 15th Infantry had dug in for the night on its newly established positions.

To lead the renewal of the 7th Infantry attack up the Ponte Rotto–Cisterna road, the 1st Battalion, 30th Infantry, was brought up from division reserve. Before it could reach the line of departure at Ponte Rotto, fourteen German tanks, some of them Tigers, attacked down the road from Cisterna. The Sherman tanks and M–10 tank destroyers swung forward to meet the attackers. They caught the enemy tanks in an exposed position along the road, unable to deploy because of the soggy fields and ditches on both sides. In the ensuing tank battle, Shermans of the 751st Tank Battalion knocked out three of the enemy tanks; a platoon of the 601st Tank Destroyer Battalion shot up two more. The infantry called for artillery fire from the 9th Field Artillery Battalion. The Germans hurriedly withdrew. Then, behind massed fires laid down by the 9th, 10th, and 41st Field Artillery Battalions, the 1st Battalion, led by Maj. Oliver G. Kenny, attacked up the road at 1620 and advanced a quarter of a mile beyond the creek before darkness forced it to dig in

On the extreme left of the 3d Division attack, the 1st Battalion, 7th Infantry, which had reorganized during 30 January, again tried to cross the railroad northwest of Cisterna and cut Highway No. 7. Major Sinsel employed his armor and heavy mortars to clean out the farmhouses and haystacks from which enemy machine guns were holding up the battalion. Against slight opposition he then pushed forward toward the railroad line. En route, the battalion surprised and overran a group of 150 Germans, who evidently had no idea American troops had penetrated so far, for they were not even dug in to meet the attack. When the battalion reached the railroad line, the situation changed. Here they were halted by dense, interlocking bands of fire from what was evidently the enemy's main line of resistance. The bridge over the railroad had been blown, preventing tanks from getting across to clean out the enemy. Under cover of the accompanying tanks and tank destroyers, whose fire drove the Germans to shelter, Major Sinsel withdrew his battalion south about 400 yards to a reverse slope and dug in for all-around defense. All night and

the next day (1 February) the Germans showered the exposed salient with artillery and mortar fire and tried to infiltrate machine guns to the battalion's flanks. Each time they heard the Germans moving in, four or five men would sneak up and knock out the enemy machine-gun crew. At 1930 the battalion drove off a counterattack on the left rear and captured two enemy machine guns. Although they had almost exhausted their ammunition and were out of contact with the other rifle companies, Major Sinsel and one hundred of his men held their positions. A strong patrol from the 2d Battalion, 7th Infantry, was hastily moved up that night to plug the gap between the 1st Battalion and Company G, 30th Infantry, and to mop up enemy snipers to their rear; it returned without having made contact with Company G.

The night of 31 January, ending the second day of the attack on Cisterna, found the 3d Division battling stubbornly forward but still unable to break through. Many fresh German units, especially mobile reconnaissance battalions, which were usually the first elements of a new division to arrive, had been committed on 31 January to reinforce the *Hermann Goering Panzer Division*. The enemy's sharply increased use of massed armor was made possible by the arrival of the bulk of the *26th Panzer Division* from the Adriatic front.

On the morning of 1 February the 3d Division renewed its effort to reach Cisterna. (Map No. 8.) Jumping off at dawn, the 1st Battalion, 30th Infantry, fought its way 1,000 yards farther up the Ponte Rotto–Cisterna road. The battalion reached Pantano ditch, less than a mile west of Cisterna, placing it about the same distance away from the town as the 15th Infantry on the south, when a well-laid 10-minute German artillery concentration forced it to halt and dig in. A German battalion, reinforced by tanks and artillery, promptly counterattacked before American troops could organize for defense. This dangerous assault was staved off largely by the heroic action of Pfc. Alton W. Knappenberger of Company C, 30th Infantry. Crawling forward with his Browning automatic rifle to an exposed knoll ahead of his unit, Private Knappenberger

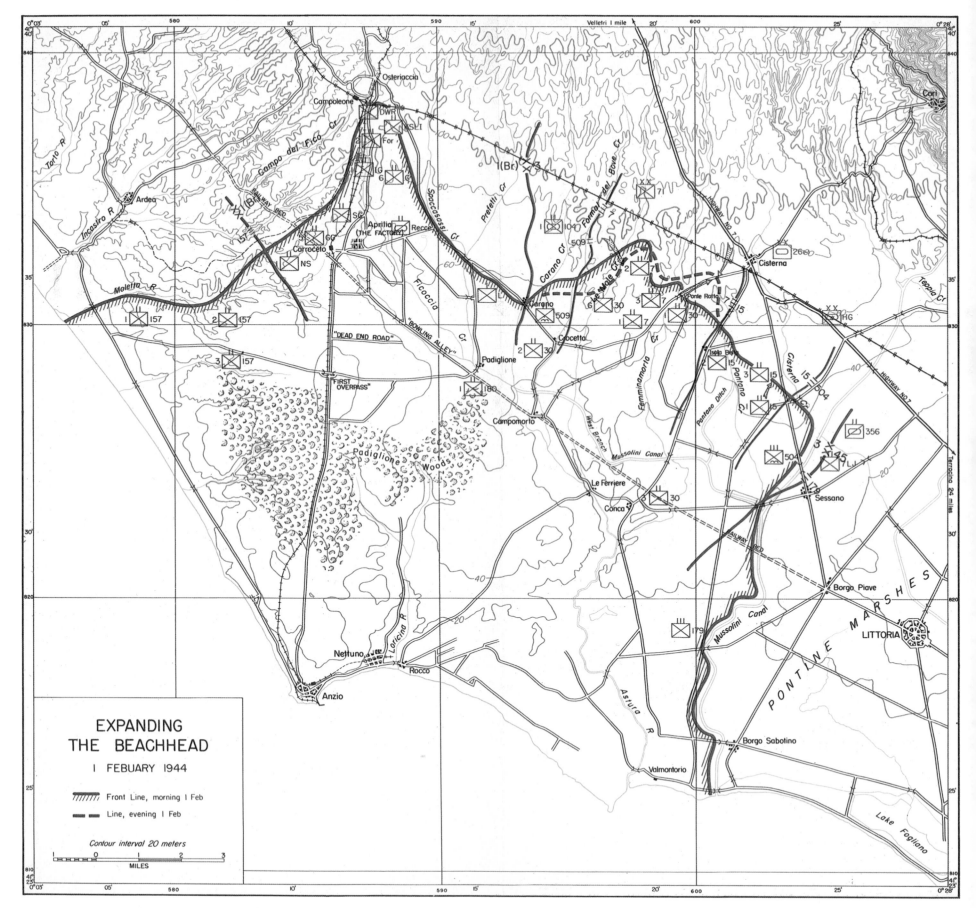

EXPANDING
THE BEACHHEAD

I FEBUARY 1944

Front Line, morning I Feb

Line, evening I Feb

Contour interval 20 meters

MILES

MAP NO. 8

held back the Germans long enough for the two advance companies of the battalion to withdraw and reorganize. With machine-gun bullets, grenades, and 20-mm. *flakwagon* shells bursting around him, he first knocked out a German machine gun, killing two and wounding another of the crew. As he did so, two Germans crept up and threw grenades within ten feet of him. Private Knappenberger killed both Germans with a burst of fire. Remaining in an exposed position throughout the action, he dispersed an entire enemy platoon. Only when his ammunition was gone did he rejoin his company 300 yards to the rear. The 1st Battalion remained near Pantano ditch where it had been stopped in its drive.

General Truscott considered it essential to protect the division right flank before any resumption of the attack on Cisterna. Accordingly, he ordered the 15th Infantry to continue its advance toward the Cisterna–Littoria road in order to block any possible enemy counterattack across Cisterna Creek. On the morning of 1 February the 1st Battalion attacked for the third time in an effort to reach the road. For the third time it failed. The troops were unable to break through the *Hermann Goering Panzer Division* barricaded in the houses barring the way.

By noon it was clear that the 3d Division, holding a wide front and exhausted by three days of bitter fighting, could not hope to take Cisterna in the face of the ever increasing build-up of enemy troops. In fact, the German concentration opposite the 3d Division, and, in particular, the appearance of the *26th Panzer Division,* the enemy's chief mobile reserve, forecast an early German counterattack. General Truscott pulled back the 1st Battalion, 30th Infantry, from its exposed position to the stream line at Ponte Rotto and ordered all troops to dig in immediately to meet the expected attack.

Meanwhile the 1st Battalion, 7th Infantry, harassed by enemy snipers, antitank guns, and constant infiltration attempts, held on precariously in its exposed salient along the railroad northwest of Cisterna. The Germans considered this wedge thrust deep into their defenses a serious threat to their position and counterattacked strongly with elements of the newly arrived *71st Infantry Division.* By the afternoon of 1 February Major Sinsel reported his battered force had to be relieved or would be forced to withdraw. When the 2d Battalion relieved the 1st that night, Company C was down to sixteen men and Company A to eighteen, though many other men had filtered back separately. The relieving battalion was scarcely in position when it was attacked at dawn on 2 February by a fresh battalion of the *26th Panzer Division.* Supporting tanks, tank destroyers, and artillery helped repulse this thrust in three hours of bitter fighting. The same enemy unit attacked again that afternoon and was again thrown back. In repelling these two attacks the Americans had smashed the entire German battalion, capturing 131 prisoners in the subsequent mop-up. The 7th Infantry still held firm.

On the afternoon of 1 February the 3d Division attack toward Cisterna had lost its momentum. In three days the division had gained two to three miles up the roads leading to Cisterna, but had been unable to break through the last 1,500 yards to seize the town. The division had fought on approximately a 7-mile front toward an objective three to four miles away. An attack on such a wide front by a limited force could be expected to succeed only against relatively weak enemy opposition. But the opposition was not weak. The Germans succeeded in building up their strength and establishing a defensive system around Cisterna in time to stem the attack. Instead of meeting mobile covering forces, 3d Division troops struck well-organized and strongly dug-in positions amply supported by artillery and armor. In spite of these obstacles, the division almost reached Cisterna, and, although it suffered heavy losses, it had also inflicted heavy losses on the Germans. By the evening of 1 February, however, the tide had turned; the enemy now had numerical superiority. Forced to assume the defensive, the 3d Division began hastily digging in behind a barrier of mines, wire, and antitank guns to hold its gains and meet the expected enemy counterthrust. An uneasy lull settled over the division front as Americans and Germans prepared for the fight to come.

## Advance to Campoleone

While General Truscott on the right drove on Cisterna, VI Corps made its main effort toward Colli Laziali along the Albano road. From the British positions above Carroceto this dominating hill mass was clearly visible. General Lucas' plan called for the British 1 Division to breach the enemy's main line of resistance along the railroad by seizing the crossing at Campoleone. The 1st Armored Division was to swing wide around to the left of the Albano road to assault Colli Laziali from the west while the British continued their attack up the main road to seize the high ground on the south slope.

The plan of General Penney, commanding the 1 Division, was to pass the fresh 3 Brigade through the 24 Guards Brigade to seize Campoleone. At 2300, 29 January, the 1 Scots Guards and the 1 Irish Guards attacked to secure the crossroads 2,000 yards south of the Campoleone overpass as a line of departure for the main attack. (Map No. 5.) The 1 Scots Guards on the right struck a mined and wired-in road block south of its objective but pushed through with heavy losses. On the left of the road, however, the 1 Irish Guards were forced back at dawn by enemy tanks and self-propelled guns. To meet the threat of enemy armor the 3d Battalion, 1st Armored Regiment, was hastily withdrawn from the 1st Armored Division attack and sent to assist the British. American and British tanks and tank destroyers drove off the enemy armor, and the infantry was able to restore its forward positions. The defending *29th Panzer Grenadier Regiment* was severely handled in this action.

The sharp fighting for the line of departure delayed the 3 Brigade attack until 1510, 30 January. (Map No. 6.) At this time the 1 Battalion, King's Shropshire Light Infantry (1 KSLI), and 1 Battalion, Duke of Wellington's Regiment (1 DWR), drove forward against scattered opposition and seized their objective on the high ground just south of the overpass at Campoleone. Tanks of the 46 Royal Tanks hotly engaged enemy antitank guns beyond the railway embankment but were unable to cross. Since it was now too dark to continue the attack across the railroad, further advance by the 1 Division was postponed until the next day.

The area west of the Albano road, chosen for the armored assault, is cut up by a series of rough stream gullies, often fifty feet deep, which run in a southwesterly direction down from the high ground to the sea. Instead of attacking across the ravines, which would offer difficult barriers to armored vehicles, Maj. Gen. Ernest R. Harmon, commander of the 1st Armored Division, planned first to seize the old railroad bed running northwest from Carroceto. The railroad bed offered a built-up route of advance across the gullies and, once gained, it could be used as a line of departure for a drive northeast along the more favorable ground of the ridges lying between the gullies.

General Harmon assigned the task of clearing the area along the old railroad bed to Col. Kent C. Lambert, commander of Combat Command A. Colonel Lambert prepared to make a reconnaissance in force, employing Company B, 81st Reconnaissance Battalion, Companies A and I, 1st Armored Regiment, the 1st Battalion, 6th Armored Infantry, and the 91st Armored Field Artillery Battalion.

This force was dispatched on the afternoon of 29 January. (Map No. 5.) In order not to interfere with priority traffic on the main Albano road, the column turned off at the first overpass and followed a track leading north to Buonriposo Ridge. The Germans were not believed to have more than small delaying forces in this area. As the leading armored cars nosed onto the ridge, they were met by sniper and machine-gun fire from enemy positions on the upper side of the Moletta River gully. Unable to cross the deep ravine, the tanks and armored cars skirted the south bank up to the railway bed, where they were halted by a mine field and by intense enemy fire. Colonel Lambert withdrew his force out of range to regroup. No sooner had the tanks halted than they bogged down in the muddy ground. Colonel Lambert decided to hold up for the night short of the railroad bed and secure the line of departure in the morning after his tanks had been dug out and suitable reconnaissance had been made.

The remainder of the 1st Armored Regiment and the 6th Armored Infantry (less the 2d Battalion, still on the southern front) moved up under cover of night to reinforce Combat Command A. (Map No. 6.) The 3d Battalion, 504th Parachute Infantry, and the 894th Tank Destroyer Battalion were attached as division reserve. Once the tanks were freed the following morning, five tank companies moved out across the upper Moletta gully and engaged the enemy along the next ridge. Many of the tanks, however, bogged down

again, and the heavy smoke and artillery fire on a cold, cloudy day made it difficult for the tankers to see. Since the armor was unable to get beyond the gravel road along the ridge, General Harmon ordered the 6th Armored Infantry under Col. Paul Steele to attack with the tanks astride the railway bed and clear out enemy resistance to the next stream line. Careful plans were worked out for tank-infantry cooperation to reduce each enemy strong point. These plans had to be partly canceled when a tank battalion (3d Battalion, 1st Armored Regiment) was withdrawn just before the attack and sent north to assist the British. Lack of this tank support hampered the assault of the 6th Armored Infantry. The infantry pushed forward that afternoon through a wall of mortar and machine-gun fire and reached the gravel road along the ridge. Here they were held until dark by a 400-yard hasty mine field, well covered by antitank guns, laid at the intersection of road and railway bed. By the end of the first day of the attack along the Albano road the 1st Armored Division was still struggling for its line of departure, and the British, while scoring a 2-mile advance, had still to breach the enemy defenses at Campoleone.

In General Lucas' original plan of attack, the British 1 Division was to drive up the Albano road to reach the south slope of Colli Laziali, while the 1st Armored Division swung around the left of the 1 Division to seize the high ground on the west slope. In view of the difficulty met by the 1st Armored Division in the muddy country and rough stream gullies west of the Albano road, General Lucas changed his plan. Instead of attacking northeast up the ridges from the railway bed, the armor was to wait until the British had taken the road junction at Osteriaccia, 1,000 yards north of Campoleone. When the crossroads had been taken, a column of the 1st Armored Regiment[1] was to pass through the British and attack up the Albano road. The 1 Division would follow as quickly as possible. Meanwhile, the 6th Armored Infantry, once more

[1] Minus the 3d Battalion but with the 3d Battalion, 504th Parachute Infantry, and 27th Armored Field Artillery Battalion attached.

with a tank battalion in support (3d Battalion, 1st Armored Regiment), was to continue its attack at dawn to seize the two and one-half miles along the railway bed designated as the line of departure in the original order, and then prepare to attack north.

At 1030, 31 January, the 2 Battalion, Sherwood Foresters (2 Foresters), and tanks of the 46 Royal Tanks attacked from their positions south of the overpass at Campoleone with the objective of seizing the crossroads at Osteriaccia and breaching the enemy line of resistance along the railroad embankment at Campoleone to allow the armor to pass through. (Map No. 7.) They fought their way across the embankment but then ran into a hornet's nest of resistance from part of the *29th Panzer Grenadier Regiment* firmly intrenched in the houses lining the road from Campoleone to Osteri-

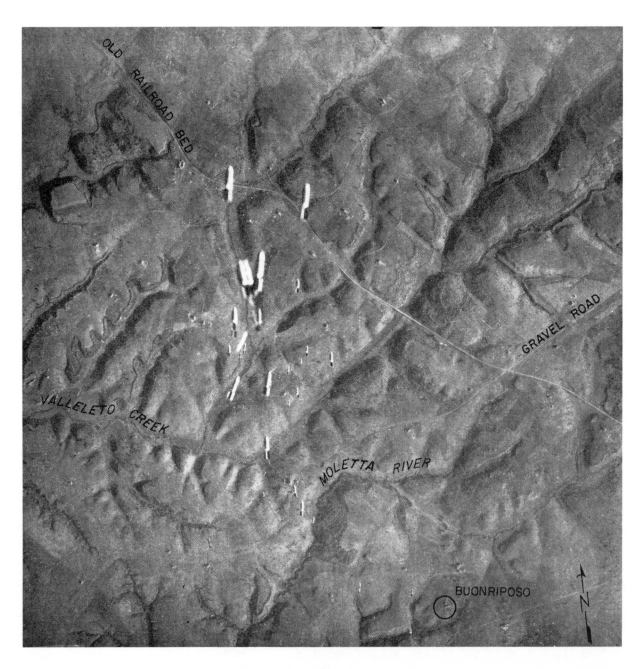

accia. Tanks and self-propelled guns covered every avenue of approach. Some of them had been driven through the backs of buildings and were firing out the windows. A mine field barred progress up the road. Brig. J. R. James, commanding the 3 Brigade, withdrew his infantry in order to allow tanks and artillery to soften up German defenses.

In preparation for the armored assault, General Harmon had ordered Maj. William R. Tuck to employ his 1st Battalion, 1st Armored Regiment, to reconnoiter the more level ground west of the Albano road near Campoleone for suitable stream crossings and routes across the railroad embankment. On the morning of 31 January, the tank column had swung up the road behind the British positions, and then had turned off and fanned out over the rise south of Campo del Fico Creek. Overrunning enemy machine gunners, they drove the Germans from the ridge. Enemy infantry counterattacked but were shot down by the tanks' machine guns. The estimated killed numbered 175. 1st Lt. Olin Dyer's platoon of Company C skirted the next gully until it found a crossing and then charged up the ridge on the far side while the Germans broke and fled. The platoon overran three mortar positions and a 75-mm. antitank gun. An enemy self-propelled gun set fire to Lieutenant Dyer's tank, but was in turn set aflame by another of his platoon. Two Mark IV's were put out of action by gunner Everett B. Perrien, using a 37-mm. gun. Having driven off the enemy tanks, the light tanks moved forward to the railroad, but were stopped by enemy antitank guns and heavy weapons along the railroad embankment. Intense enemy artillery fire throughout the action was largely ineffective because of the high percentage of air burst, which rattled off the buttoned-up tanks. Unable to force their way across the embankment before dark, the American tanks withdrew.

As a prelude to a renewed British attack on the afternoon of 31 January, the 2d Battalion, 1st Armored Regiment, launched a raid up the Albano road toward Campoleone. The medium tanks reached the railroad embankment and fired heavily on the fortified houses beyond at about a 700-yard range but were unable to cross because of severe enemy fire. After a massed artilley preparation by the 1 Division artillery, the 2 Foresters attacked again, but were turned back by heavy small-arms, mortar, and self-propelled gun fire from enemy positions some 300 yards beyond the railway. The effort of the 1st Armored and 1 Divisions to break through along the Albano road had not succeeded.

While the drive on Campoleone was in progress, the 6th Armored Infantry had resumed its attack along the old railroad bed northwest of Carroceto at dawn on 31 January. The battalion met heavy machine-gun fire from Germans intrenched in farmhouses across its line of advance. Essential tank support to knock out these German strong points was delayed in coming up; and the mine fields, barring the way up the railroad bed, proved to be well covered by German antitank guns which Allied artillery was unable to knock out. Against strong opposition and unusually heavy German artillery fire, the troops were able to gain only 500 yards. By evening, Colonel Steele reported that a further advance would be extremely difficult. His flanks were unprotected and his center was held up where the mine field had not been cleared. General Harmon halted the attack and the 6th Armored Infantry and its supporting tanks were relieved by the 24 Brigade that night. VI Corps withdrew the 1st Armored Division back into Corps reserve.

The Allied attack (British 1 Division supported by British and American armor) toward Campoleone had made better progress than the 3d Division drive on Cisterna. It had reached Campoleone,

ZONE OF ARMORED ATTACK ON THE LEFT FLANK *was over the ridges and gullies of the Moletta River, Valleleto Creek, and their tributaries. Photographed from a high-level bomber during a mission against German positions in the ridges, the gravel road where the tanks were halted and the railroad bed are seen clearly.*

and penetrated the German main line of resistance west of the Albano road, where a 2-mile gap was opened between the *65th Infantry Division* on the west and the *3d Panzer Grenadier Division* holding the center of the German line east of Campoleone. Despite this Allied penetration along the Albano road, which became known as the Campoleone salient, by 1 February the VI Corps attack to secure Cisterna and Campoleone had spent itself against unexpectedly strong German defenses. Reconnaissance reports before the offensive had indicated that the Germans held only delaying positions before Cisterna and Campoleone, and that their main line of resistance lay back on the high ground of Colli Laziali and the Lepini Mountains. Instead, the Germans determined to make their stand before Cisterna and Campoleone, key points on the two main axes of attack inland.

The enemy had not only succeeded in rushing up reinforcements in wholly unexpected strength, but had also built up a strong system of defenses barring the approaches to Cisterna and Campoleone. Every house and village was converted into a strong point and these were connected by well-camouflaged machine-gun nests and rifle pits. Tanks and roving self-propelled guns and massed artillery and *nebelwerfer* fire supported these positions. Allied troops again found, as they had all through the Italian campaign, the excellent fortification value of the heavy stone construction of Italian farmhouses. Reducing each house was in fact a small separate operation, requiring tanks and tank destroyers to demolish the building before the infantry could move in. Sniping and infiltration by small enemy groups continued long after key defense points were seized, and the infantry continually had to mop up bypassed pockets of Germans who fired on them from the rear.

Every advantage of terrain, too, lay with the enemy. On the left flank the armor found it difficult to penetrate the natural obstacles presented by rough stream gullies and ground made soggy by repeated rains. On the right flank the route of advance lay over open, muddy fields offering scant cover for the attacker while providing excellent fields of fire for defending troops. January rains made ground movement difficult, and low clouds during the crucial period of the attack severely hampered the air effort. In the face of such a combination of obstacles, Allied troops had driven fourteen miles inland from Anzio to within five miles of Colli Laziali, but they lacked the strength to break through at Cisterna and Campoleone.

After a conference with General Clark on 1 February, General Alexander ordered VI Corps to continue the attack to extend the beachhead to the Incastro River–Campoleone–Cisterna line, and then organize for defense. The initial beachhead had been the largest that could be held with the limited number of troops originally landed, but it was so small that any part could be reached by enemy artillery and there was little room for maneuver or defense in depth. A breakthrough at any point would bring the Germans almost to the sea. Consequently General Alexander desired to extend the beachhead farther inland and anchor it on the key points of Cisterna and Campoleone. By the afternoon of 1 February, however, it was evident that these objectives could not immediately be attained. The enemy build-up had become so threatening that VI Corps ordered all divisions to organize to repel a counterattack. On 2 February, General Clark radioed General Lucas to consolidate the beachhead and prepare for defense. General Lucas on 3 February gave verbal orders to the units of VI Corps to assume the defensive. All units began immediate preparations of defensive positions to meet the expected German assault.

In anticipation of the enemy offensive, Allied reinforcements were sped to the beachhead to offset the growing German superiority of force. The 1st Special Service Force, a mixed brigade of 1,800 picked Canadians and Americans, arrived on 2 February and took over the right flank along the main Mussolini Canal. The 168 Brigade of the British 56 Division landed at the beachhead on 3 February to reinforce the British. Antiaircraft and heavy artillery were strongly reinforced to meet the constant Luftwaffe raids and the growing menace of long-range guns. By 4 February, the strength of

VI Corps had increased to nearly 100,000, including service troops. Although inferior to the enemy in numbers of troops,[2] it was better equipped and supplied—particularly in guns and ammunition—than the opposing German forces.

While the Allied offensive of 30 January–1 February made only one important penetration, the German *Fourteenth Army* was forced to commit the bulk of its combat forces to stem the VI Corps advance. In fact, Allied armor came very close to effecting a breakthrough at Campoleone Station on 31 January. For the time being, *Fourteenth Army* had to postpone a large-scale counterattack designed to wipe out the Allied beachhead, and to

_____
[2] It is estimated that *Fourteenth Army* numbered about 110,000 at this time.

limit its immediate mission to defense—preventing the Allied troops from expanding their beachhead and inflicting on them as heavy losses as possible. On 1 February *Fourteenth Army* for the first time expressed doubt that it had sufficient strength to eliminate the Anzio beachhead. The German losses in the fighting of 30–31 January were heavy. Allied bombings of railroad lines were delaying the arrival of reserves; more importantly, they were preventing the Germans from receiving an adequate supply of ammunition. Nevertheless, *Fourteenth Army* was ordered to hold assault troops in readiness to launch a counteroffensive at the first opportune moment.

The Germans expected that VI Corps would continue its offensive on 1 February, with the main

CAMPOLEONE STATION *was the farthest point of advance in the initial drive out of the beachhead. Looking south over the open, muddy flatlands, the only prominent feature in the plain is the Factory.*

HIGHWAY    RAILROAD    THE FACTORY

effort in the bulge north of the Factory, but this did not materialize. The Germans themselves counterattacked strongly west of Cisterna at dawn on 1 February with the *71st Infantry Division* and the *Hermann Goering Panzer Division.* But German attempts on 1–2 February to recover their former forward positions in front of their main line of resistance were repulsed. In effect, VI Corps in its offensive had advanced its positions up to the German main line of resistance along the whole beachhead perimeter, and penetrated it in the bulge up the Anzio–Albano road. On 2 February the Germans were also forced to draw back their main line of resistance in the *71st Infantry Division* sector north of Carano; this division had suffered heavy losses and had to shorten its front in order to strengthen its position.

As soon as VI Corps halted its offensive after three days of heavy fighting, *Fourteenth Army* renewed preparations for a major counterattack. The weight and accuracy of Allied artillery fire delayed this attack. The Germans attributed the partial failure of the counterattack launched by the *Hermann Goering Panzer Division* on 1–2 February to the demoralizing effect of Allied artillery fire. On 2 February, the artillery communications net of *Combat Group Graeser* was totally destroyed; the loss of fire direction charts forced a 24-hour postponement of the counterattack on the bulge north of the Factory. On 2 February also, *Army Group C* ordered the transfer of troops to meet the threatened invasion at Civitavecchia, and announced its intention of transferring some troops

from *Fourteenth Army* to bolster the Cassino front. Such factors were to limit the German counterattack on 3 February to a preliminary drive against the bulge north of the Factory, and require a postponement of the major German counteroffensive to 16 February.

The projected main Fifth Army drive against Cassino and the strongly defended mountain mass to its rear was launched on 1 February. During the first week of February the troops of II Corps penetrated the mountain defenses of the Gustav Line and fought into Cassino itself. But they could not break through the final German positions and reach the Liri Valley. After 7 February, despite successive assaults during the remainder of the month by American, New Zealand, and Indian troops, there was but slight forward progress in the Cassino drive; at the end of the month, a virtual stalemate had developed. Elsewhere on the Fifth and Eighth Army fronts, bad weather, and a decision to await the outcome of the critical action at Cassino, led to a postponement of all large-scale offensive operations after the beginning of February. Thus the projected plan to coordinate a drive out of the Anzio beachhead with an advance on the southern front came to naught. During the critical days of the Anzio campaign in mid-February, operations on the southern front, except at Cassino, were at a standstill. Because of this stalemate in the south, the enemy was able to hold the Fifth and Eighth Armies at bay with fewer troops than he assembled before Anzio in an all-out effort to drive VI Corps from its beachhead.

# THE ENEMY ATTACKS
# (3-12 February)

At the beginning of February General Macken-sen's *Fourteenth Army* was preparing to strike. Hitler had personally ordered that the "abscess" below Rome be removed, whatever the cost. Having stopped the Allied drive toward Cisterna and Campoleone, the Germans renewed their preparations for an all-out offensive against the Anzio beachhead. For the first two weeks of February, while these preparations were under way, the Germans believed that VI Corps might again attack toward Cisterna and Campoleone in an effort to break out of the beachhead. They also thought that the Allies might attempt another amphibious landing northwest of Anzio, and coordinate it with a drive from the beachhead area across the Moletta River to the northwest. The German attacks of early February were designed not only to pave the way for the enemy's main offensive but also, by maintaining constant pressure on VI Corps, to prevent the Allies from reorganizing for a new drive out of the beachhead.

The situation and mission of *Fourteenth Army* was summarized on 3 February in its Journal as follows:

*Fourteenth Army* intends to prevent the enlarging of the beachhead, and to prepare an attack to eliminate this area. A number of army units are remnants from various organizations and are not able to mount an attack at this time; during the last days, they had to be used in the front lines to prevent any enemy breakthrough. With these forces a strong assault group to conduct the attack on the beachhead cannot be organized. Therefore, *Fourteenth Army* has planned attacks with limited objectives,

to suit various situations as they arise. When the enemy is weakened by these attacks, an all-out counteroffensive will be launched.

At the same time, *Fourteenth Army* headquarters again expressed doubt that the Anzio beachhead could be eliminated with the forces then available to it, and requested *Army Group C* to attach additional troops in order that the ultimate mission of eliminating the beachhead might be accomplished.

On the eve of their first large-scale offensive, the Germans reorganized their forces. *I Parachute Corps,* which had previously commanded the entire Anzio front under *Fourteenth Army,* was assigned the western sector from a point west of the Albano road to the sea behind the Moletta River. It had two divisions under its command, the *4th Parachute* on the west and the *65th Infantry* on the east. The staff of *LXXVI Panzer Corps* was transferred from *Tenth Army* in the south, where it had commanded the enemy forces opposing the British Eighth Army, to *Fourteenth Army,* and given control over the central and eastern sectors of the beachhead perimeter. It took over its new command at 1200, 4 February. Five divisions were placed under it; in order, from the Albano road eastward, they were the *3d Panzer Grenadier,* the *715th Infantry* (motorized), the *71st Infantry,* and the *Hermann Goering Panzer Divisions,* together with the *26th Panzer Division,* most of which was held in Corps reserve. In practice, German attacks were usually launched by combat groups that were formed by varying combinations of units. The most important of these, *Combat Group Graeser,* was to spearhead the enemy attacks against the center of the beachhead line.

The VI Corps offensive at the end of January had concentrated on two areas: the roads leading northeast from Anzio to Cisterna and the paved highway running north from Anzio toward Albano. These avenues, which traversed the only terrain suitable to the employment of tanks and heavy equipment, were likewise the most favorable routes for an enemy attack to drive VI Corps into the sea.

The German offensive against the Anzio beachhead launched in February had three principal phases: first, preparatory attacks to pinch off the deep British salient up the Albano road and capture the important Factory area (3–10 February); second, a major drive to break through to the sea along the axis of the Albano road (16–20 February); and third, an attack on the Cisterna front aimed at the main Allied beachhead defense line along the Mussolini Canal (28 February–2 March). The first of these attacks was to succeed; the second and third were to be repulsed by Allied forces that held grimly to the beachhead area and preserved it as a springboard for the subsequent offensive that led to the capture of Rome.

## Battle of the Campoleone Salient

On the night of 3–4 February the Germans began their Anzio offensive by launching a two-pronged assault from the west and east against the center of the deep Allied salient extending up the Albano road from Carroceto to Campoleone. This attack was the first step in a preliminary offensive to capture the Factory–Carroceto area, which commanded the road network leading to Anzio and Nettuno; this area was to be the position for a jump-off in the major German drive that was to follow. (Map No. 9.)

The drive launched on 30 January by the Allied 1st Armored and 1 Divisions up the Albano road had created a narrow salient approximately three miles deep and from one to one and one-half miles wide. If the Germans could pinch off the British

units holding this salient, they would achieve the destruction of a sizable portion of the beachhead forces and at the same time open the way for further attacks down the Albano road. Quick to seize the opportunity, the enemy rushed troops into position for the attack.

After the Allied advance was stopped on 1 February, the 1st Armored Division was withdrawn into Corps reserve, leaving the British 1 Division occupying the ground which had been won. The apex of the salient just south of the railroad at Campoleone was held by the entire 3 Infantry Brigade consisting of the 1 DWR, the 2 Foresters, and the 1 KSLI. On the left flank of the salient and echeloned to the southwest was the 24 Guards Brigade consisting, in order of position, of the 1 Battalion, Irish Guards, the 1 Scots Guards, and the 5 Grenadier Guards, with the 2 North Stafford-shire Regiment (2 North Staffs) attached. The 2 North Staffs were in contact with the 157th Infantry Regiment, 45th Division, defending the Moletta River line on the left flank of the beachhead. On the right flank of the salient, and echeloned to the southeast, was the 2 Infantry Brigade (less the 2 North Staffs), consisting of the 6 Battalion, Gordon Highlanders (6 Gordons), and the 1 Battalion, Loyal Regiment (1 Loyals) reinforced in the center by elements of the 1 Reconnaissance Regiment (1 Recce Regiment). The 1 Loyals on the right were in contact with the 509th Parachute Infantry Battalion, near the village of Carano. The 1 Division, holding a front of approximately ten miles, had had little time to prepare for the impending attack.

To add to the difficulties of this extremely long front and an exposed salient, the terrain generally favored the enemy. West of the Albano road the maze of deep, brush-covered ravines, which had proved such an obstacle to the tanks of the 1st Armored Division, offered the enemy concealed assembly areas from which they could infiltrate between the isolated strong points held by the British troops. East of the Albano road the country is more open, but the road leading southeast from Osteriaccia toward Carano offered enemy tanks

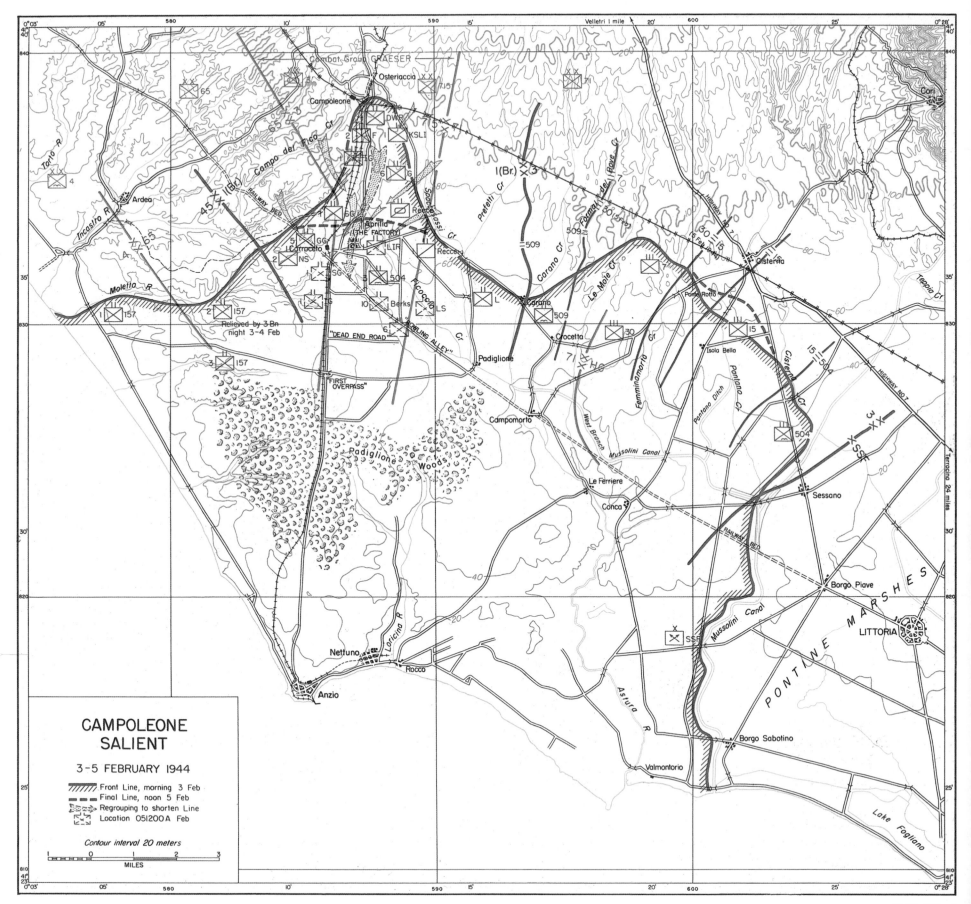

CAMPOLEONE
SALIENT

3–5 FEBRUARY 1944

Front Line, morning 3 Feb
Final Line, noon 5 Feb
Regrouping to shorten Line
Location 051200A Feb

Contour interval 20 meters

MILES

MAP NO. 9

an avenue of approach from concealed assembly points behind the railroad embankment east of Campoleone.

Late in the afternoon of 3 February the enemy laid an artillery concentration on the positions of the 1 DWR southwest of the railroad and followed it with a small infantry attack. This proved to be only a diversion involving not more than a company. Artillery fire broke up the attack and by dark the slight enemy penetration had been wiped out. Then, shortly before midnight, the enemy artillery opened up again. This time the fire was concentrated near the base of the salient with the heaviest fire falling in the sector east of the Albano road. At 2300 the 1 Irish Guards west of the highway reported enemy troops infiltrating between their positions and those of the 1 Scots Guards on their left. At 2330 the 6 Gordons on the east side of the salient also were under attack. Enemy units also struck at the 1 KSLI and 1 DWR at the nose of the salient. In the confusion of night fighting it was difficult to measure the strength of the attacks, but by dawn the enemy's intention was clear. By driving deep wedges into both sides of the salient near its base, he aimed to cut off the whole of the 3 Brigade.

At daybreak on 4 February the attack on the west appeared to be the more threatening. An enemy battalion of the *65th Infantry Division,* supported by a few tanks and self-propelled guns, broke through the left flank of the 1 Irish Guards to reach the Campoleone–Nettuno railroad paralleling the Albano road. Later it became evident that the more serious threat was to the east flank of the salient. At 0725 at least six enemy tanks were spotted near a farmhouse to the east of the 6 Gordons. Swinging west along a dirt road, the tanks overran one company of the 6 Gordons and established themselves on a small ridge just east of the Albano road. Infantry poured in behind the tanks, antitank guns were brought up, and additional tanks moved in to complete the isolation of the 3 Brigade. This attack was launched by *Combat Group Graeser,* and spearheaded by the *104th Panzer Grenadier Regiment* reinforced by three additional infantry battalions, two artillery battalions, two combat engineer companies, and armor, including Mark V (Panther) tanks.

FARMHOUSE ATTACKED IN THE BRITISH ZONE. *British troops holding the line west of the Albano road were operating over terrain where observation was difficult. This farmhouse on a ridge was photographed early in the Anzio campaign and was in use as an observation post. Constant shelling reduced most such structures.*

As the morning wore on the situation became increasingly difficult for the 1 Irish Guards and the 6 Gordons. Sherman tanks of the 46 Royal Tank Regiment, counterattacking to support the 1 Irish Guards, were outranged by the enemy's tanks and heavy antitank guns which had been emplaced to cover the Albano road. The 1 Irish Guards fell back to the southeast taking up a hedgehog position for all-around defense. Isolated by the enemy penetration, the 3 Brigade in the apex of the salient was under constant attack. Fighting under leaden skies and drizzling rain, it could not count on air support. By noon the situation seemed critical. General Penney, commander of the 1 Division, ordered the 168 Infantry Brigade (British 56 Division) to alert one battalion for a possible counterattack.

During the afternoon of 4 February the force of the enemy attacks gradually weakened against the stubborn defense put up by the 24 Guards Brigade and the 6 Gordons. By 1500 the 1 Irish Guards had fought its way out of the trap created by the penetration on the left flank; the 6 Gordons continued to hold the ground south of the ridge line; and in the beleaguered 3 Brigade area the 1 KSLI successfully intercepted a party of Germans escorting 100 British prisoners. Enemy tanks and infantry suffered from accurate artillery and tank-destroyer fire. Company C, 894th Tank Destroyer Battalion, knocked out four enemy tanks and an antitank gun which the German crew was man-handling into position; Company B picked off one Mark IV tank. At 1600, when the force of the enemy attacks showed signs of weakening, the 1 London Scottish (168 Brigade), supported by tanks of the 46 Royal Tanks, launched a counterattack. Suffering heavy losses, the enemy was forced to fall back, and by 1700 the gap between the 6 Gordons and the 3 Brigade had been wiped out.

Although the initial German attack had been checked, General Lucas considered that the forward units of the 1 Division were dangerously exposed, and he ordered them withdrawn to a new and more defensible line. The 1 KSLI and the 2 Foresters drew back quickly with only slight losses. The 1 DWR, which was under direct fire from enemy tanks, was unable to extricate itself until after dark; one company had been cut off, and the remainder of the battalion had to leave behind most of its antitank guns and heavy equipment.

During the night of 4–5 February the 1 Division continued the withdrawal of its forward units to a line approximately a mile north of Carroceto and the Factory. The fresh 168 Brigade was moved forward to take over the center of the line and the 3 Brigade moved into division reserve. Although the readjustment of the 1 Division positions represented a loss of two and one-half miles of hard-won ground, the new line was considerably shorter and more defensible. Of the 3 Brigade units at the apex of the salient only the 1 DWR suffered heavily, the chief losses being sustained by the 1 Irish Guards, 24 Brigade, and the 6 Gordons, 2 Brigade, who had borne the brunt of the enemy's attacks at the base of the salient. Total British casualties in this action were more than 1,400 killed, wounded, and missing; the enemy claimed the capture of more than 900 prisoners.

The enemy's objective of wiping out the Campoleone salient had been achieved; his effort to isolate and destroy the 3 Brigade had largely failed. Bad weather had hampered the movement of tanks and other heavy equipment and stubborn Allied resistance had slowed down the enemy infantry attacks. The enemy had suffered heavy casualties—nearly five hundred killed—and during the operation the British took more than three hundred prisoners, most of them captured during the counterattack launched by the 1 London Scottish and the 46 Royal Tank Regiment. Prisoners reported that their units had been hit hard. One battalion was practically wiped out, and the *104th Panzer Grenadier Regiment,* which had led the attack against the 6 Gordons, was seriously depleted. Prisoners complained that the attack had been hurriedly organized without adequate reconnaissance of the ground and that some units had been moved up by forced night marches and thrown directly into the battle.

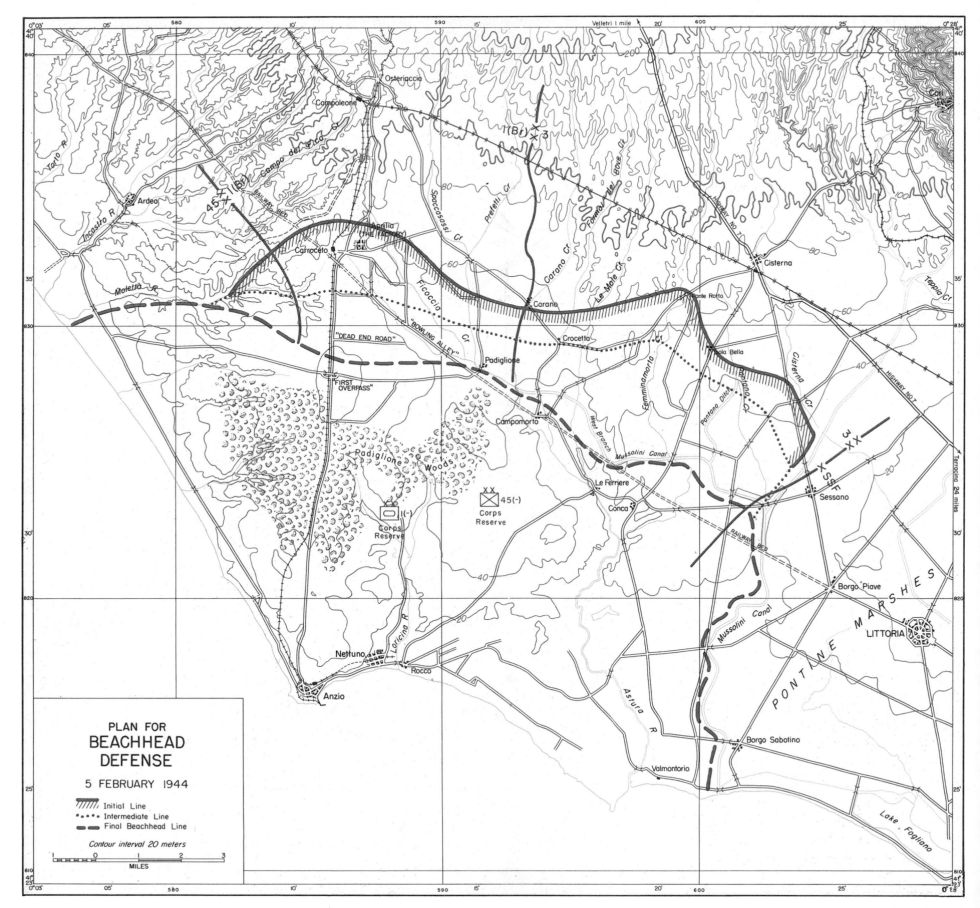

PLAN FOR
**BEACHHEAD
DEFENSE**

5 FEBRUARY 1944

▨▨▨ Initial Line
•••• Intermediate Line
▬ ▬ Final Beachhead Line

Contour interval 20 meters

MILES

MAP NO. 10

## The Beachhead Defense

On the morning of 4 February, when the fighting in the Campoleone salient was at its height, VI Corps issued written orders outlining the Corps plan of defense for the beachhead and confirming oral orders given the previous day. The initial beachhead line, which ran from the Moletta River on the left flank across the open fields of the central sector to the west branch of the Mussolini Canal and south along the main canal to the sea, was to be fortified as the final beachhead line of resistance. During the period of the expansion of the beachhead VI Corps had pushed out in the central sector an average of from two to four miles, with the Campoleone salient extending six miles north up the Albano road. It was the intention of VI Corps to hold the ground which had been won, falling back to the final beachhead line only as a last resort. (Map No. 10.)

The flanks of the beachhead, the Moletta River on the left and the main Mussolini Canal on the right, were considered easily defensible. The 45th Division was assigned the task of preparing defenses along the Moletta River and of holding it with one regimental combat team; responsibility for the right flank went to the 1st Special Service Force.[1] The critical central sector north of the final beachhead line was to be prepared for defense and held by the 1 Division and the 3d Division. The 1 Division (reinforced) was to be responsible for the area extending from west of the Albano road to the village of Carano.[2] The 3d Division (reinforced) would hold the area from Carano to the junction of the west branch with the main Mussolini Canal.[3] The 1st Armored Division[4] (less Com-

bat Command B) and the bulk of the 45th Division[5] were to be held in Corps reserve prepared to counterattack on Corps order. The 1st Armored Division was located east of the Albano road in the extensive area of tangled undergrowth, scrub trees, and bogland known as Padiglione Woods; in addition to its counterattack role it was to organize defenses south of the final defense line behind the 1 Division. The bulk of the 45th Division, located northeast of Nettuno along the road to Cisterna, was to organize the area south of the west branch of the Mussolini Canal behind the 3d Division. The 36th and 39th Engineer Combat Regiments, in addition to their engineer functions, were to assist in defending the coastline against airborne and seaborne raids and were to be prepared to assemble on four hours' notice as Corps reserve. At the port, the 540th Engineers, which passed to Army control on 6 February when Fifth Army took over control of supply at the beachhead, was to defend X-Ray and Nettuno beaches. During the critical days of February the task of improving the defenses absorbed the energies of every available man on the beachhead.

The enemy attack on the Campoleone salient required some changes in the plan of defense. The 168 Brigade, originally designated as Corps reserve, was committed to the support of the 1 Division, and the forward line to be consolidated was drawn back to form an arc covering the Factory area. On 5 February VI Corps designated an intermediate line approximately halfway between the initial outpost and final beachhead lines. During the month of February, although powerful enemy attacks tore deep rents in the forward lines of defense, necessitating frequent shifts in the positions of the defending troops, the general outline of the VI Corps plan of defense remained intact.

The work of preparing the defenses was performed under the most trying conditions. All operations had to be conducted at night and sometimes in the midst of battle. In the forward areas the extent of the outpost line and the relatively small

---

[1] Attached: 456th Parachute Field Artillery Battalion (less Batteries C and D).

[2] Attached: 2 Field Regiment, Royal Artillery; 3d Battalion, 504th Parachute Infantry; 168 Brigade; 46 Royal Tanks; Companies B and C, 894th Tank Destroyer Battalion.

[3] Attached: 601st Tank Destroyer Battalion; 751st Tank Battalion; 191st Tank Battalion; 441st AAA Automatic Weapons Battalion; 84th Chemical Battalion; 69th Armored Field Artillery Battalion; 504th Parachute Infantry (minus 3d Bn); 6615th Ranger Force (Provisional); 509th Parachute Infantry Battalion.

[4] Attached: 434th AAA Automatic Weapons Battalion.

[5] Attached: 645th Tank Destroyer Battalion; 894th Tank Destroyer Battalion (less Companies B and C).

FORWARD OBSERVATIONS POSTS *on the right flank usually centered in a building such as this, where tanks could find cover. The tanks not only provided armored protection but also contained powerful radio equipment, and carried enough supplies to permit the observers to remain away from the rear areas for several days.*

size of the defending force made it necessary to depend almost entirely on a system of mutually supporting strong points. The stone farmhouses that dotted the countryside played an important role in the defense. Upper floors provided sniper positions and observation posts over the relatively level and almost featureless terrain; ground floors, strengthened with sandbags and timbers, provided protection for dug-in machine guns and antitank guns. Positions were wired in and protected by antitank and antipersonnel mine fields, roads were cratered, and key bridges were prepared for demolition. Engineers of the 10th Engineer Battalion strung barbed wire in the bed of the west branch of the Mussolini Canal and then, to increase its effectiveness as a tank obstacle, built earth dams to raise the water level. Tank destroyers and supporting tanks, moving into prepared positions after dark,

helped to bolster the thinly held forward positions against the enemy's favorite tactic of night infiltration. Rudimentary in the early days of February, the defenses became increasingly effective as the weeks went by.

General Clark inspected the entire beachhead front on 6 February, visiting each of the major units of VI Corps. He found the situation quiet and fairly well in hand. There appeared to be a weak spot at the boundary between the 1 Division and the 3d Division. To strengthen this point, where the enemy line was barely two miles from the final beachhead line of defense, two battalions of the 180th Infantry (45th Division) were sent to the villages of Carano and Padiglione to prepare defenses. The 1 Division had lost a large number of antitank guns in the fighting at Campoleone, and both the 1 Division and the 3d Division were badly in need of replacements. The 3d Division alone needed 2,400 men. Every effort was made to expedite the shipment of replacements and to keep VI Corps units up to strength, but the problem remained a chronic one throughout the month of February. The absorption of large numbers of troops who had had no combat experience was difficult for units which were almost constantly in the line and often fighting desperately to hold their positions. General Clark was convinced that in order to build up an adequate force to defend the beachhead and to give it the strength necessary for future offensive operations an additional British brigade group or American regimental combat team and another 155-mm. gun battalion were

needed. Although VI Corps was now committed to a defensive role, the possibility that it would soon be in position to resume the offensive was not neglected. Fifth Army Operations Instruction No. 15, dated 7 February, which confirmed previous oral orders that VI Corps was to hold its present position, included the provision that plans were to be drawn up for a possible attack out of the beachhead toward Velletri or Albano.

After the 1 Division had successfully extricated itself from the Campoleone salient on the night of 4 February, the enemy made no large-scale attacks for three days. It was not, however, a period of inactivity. Every part of the beachhead was subject to shelling from enemy long-range guns as well

WIRE-LAYING CREWS *seldom had an opportunity to work in daylight unless smoke screens were used, as shown in this photo. Here men of the 2d Battalion, 39th Engineer Regiment, stretch accordian wire parallel to two barriers of wire on posts. Mines also were placed in the area.*

as to air attack, and while reorganizing his forces to continue the offensive the enemy made repeated efforts to feel out the new beachhead defenses. The most important of these probing attacks was launched against the 3d Division on the night of 5 February.

While the British troops in the Campoleone salient were bearing the brunt of the first German attack, the 3d Division had been reorganizing its units and preparing its defenses in depth along the initial outpost line, intermediate line, and final beachhead line based on the Mussolini Canal. The division sector was divided between the 30th Infantry on the left, the 15th Infantry in the center, and the 504th Parachute Infantry on the right, with the 7th Infantry in division reserve. The bulk of the division strength had been withdrawn to rush work on the intermediate and final defense lines, leaving only mixed holding forces along the initial outpost line.

In the sector held by the 30th Infantry the outpost line extended in an arc from the village of Carano across the open fields and deep ditches of the rolling farmland west of Cisterna to the stream crossing at Ponte Rotto. It was lightly manned by platoon-sized units of the 509th Parachute Infantry Battalion on the left; a platoon each of Companies G and F, 30th Infantry, in the center; and platoons of the 2d and 3d Battalions, 7th Infantry, and the 1st Battalion, 30th Infantry, on the right. The defenses of these positions were not yet completed. Company F, 30th Infantry, had planned to wire in its position the previous night but had been pinned down by enemy machine-gun fire. Wire communication between units was still being laid, and the troops were being reorganized.

Just at dark on the evening of 5 February the enemy put down a short, intense concentration of artillery, mortar, and tank fire on a front of two and one-half miles extending from Formal del Bove Creek to Ponte Rotto. Tanks moved up on the flanks and poured direct fire into the positions of the 2d Battalion, 7th Infantry, to the north of Ponte Rotto. Then, making liberal use of flares and machine-pistol fire, the enemy attacked. At 2125 the 2d Battalion, 7th Infantry, reported it could not hold out much longer. The platoons of Companies F and G drew back; the platoon of Company E became disorganized; and the 3d Battalion, 7th Infantry, also withdrew from its positions near Ponte Rotto. The platoons of Companies F and G, 30th Infantry, finding their right flank exposed, fell back 1,500 yards to the intermediate line. The result of this wholesale withdrawal was to produce a gap extending over nearly the whole length of the 30th Infantry sector of the outpost line. To restore the situation Company K, 30th Infantry, was ordered forward to counterattack. Supported by tanks and tank destroyers, Company K moved up the road toward Ponte Rotto. It met only light artillery and mortar fire and, with other units, regained the former forward positions of the 30th Infantry by 0230. The 3d Battalion, 7th Infantry, also counterattacked and regained its former position by 0435. The 2d Battalion, 7th Infantry, moved to the rear to reorganize; its positions were taken over by the 3d Battalion, 30th Infantry. By morning, with the exception of Ponte Rotto, the original outpost line had been restored.

The exact size of the enemy force making the attack is not known. It is probable that it represented not more than a reinforced infantry battalion supported by tanks. By clever psychological use of concentrated machine-pistol fire and flares the enemy had created the illusion of an attack in greater force. Two hours after the attack had been launched, the enemy had withdrawn. Except for heavy losses sustained by the 2d Battalion, 7th Infantry, little damage had been done.

Although American troops had lost Ponte Rotto, they profited by the lesson. The transition from offensive to defensive fighting was not easy for troops accustomed to doing the attacking; in the early days of February, officers and men had to learn many lessons the hard way. To strengthen the thinly held forward lines, General Truscott ordered tank destroyers and tanks to be placed well forward where they could provide direct support. The positions of the units on the outpost line were further improved when, on the night of 7–8 February, the division relieved the units constructing defenses along the Mussolini Canal and returned them to regimental control. This permitted the 15th and 30th Infantry and 504th Parachute Infantry to defend their respective forward areas with two battalions, keeping one in reserve. The 7th Infantry, in division reserve, continued the work of improving the defenses along the canal with the assistance of the 10th Engineer Battalion and the 39th Engineers.

In addition to probing attacks the Germans built up their artillery and increased the tempo of their shelling throughout the first two weeks of February. On 5 February, the enemy had 372 artillery pieces, with 152 of calibers exceeding 105-mm., concentrated around the Anzio beachhead. Directed by observers on the dominating heights of Colli Laziali, the Lepini Mountains, and a water tower at Littoria, the enemy's long-range artillery weap-

ons and 210-mm. and 240-mm. railroad guns could drop shells into any part of the limited beachhead area.

Air photos taken on 6 February, the first clear day in a week of bad weather, revealed the increase in enemy artillery strength. The main concentration was in the center, below Colli Laziali, where the guns could support an attack either down the Albano road or from Cisterna. A large build-up was also noted on the left flank. On the afternoon of 5 February the air strip at Nettuno was heavily shelled. Five Spitfires were destroyed, and the field had to be abandoned as a permanent base. Thereafter planes used the field only during the day, returning each night to bases near Naples. On 7 February a heavy-caliber railroad gun was reported emplaced near Campoleone. Reconnaissance planes discovered additional heavy guns on the slopes of Colli Laziali: 170-mm. guns were located on the

CAMOUFLAGED ARTILLERY POSITIONS *were improved along the Mussolini Canal as the 3d Division turned to the defensive early in February. Using the sloping west bank of the canal, the troops dug in everything they had, including weapons, supplies, and equipment.*

edge of a cliff near Lake Nemi, and a railroad gun was spotted near the mouth of a tunnel at Albano. Although the shelling from these long-range weapons was seldom accurate, the rear areas of the beachhead were so congested that material damage and casualties were inevitable. The shelling seriously delayed the work of unloading supplies in the port during this period.

As many of the enemy's heavy guns were out of range of the 155-mm. guns in Corps artillery, the Navy and Air Force were called upon to assist in knocking them out. On 5 February the cruiser U.S.S. *Brooklyn* and three destroyers were employed against guns and enemy positions on the left flank of the beachhead. Two P–51 Mustangs of the 111th Reconnaissance Squadron directed the fire of naval guns with good results. The program was repeated on the left and right flanks of the beachhead whenever the weather was favorable. In order to hamper enemy observation of the right side of the beachhead, XII Air Support Command sent P–40's and A–36's to attack the water tower at Littoria on 7 February. The next day railroad guns west of Albano were bombed. Hits on the track and a burst of yellow flame and smoke from the target area indicated that some damage had been done.

Damage from enemy bombing was much more serious than the long-range artillery fire. Day or night, the beachhead was never safe from enemy planes, which came in to bomb and strafe shipping in the harbor, the dock areas, ammunition dumps, and troop assembly areas. The enemy used an increasingly larger percentage of antipersonnel "butterfly" bombs in his night attacks, which caused casualties throughout the beachhead.

DESTRUCTION OF EQUIPMENT IN NETTUNO *as well as elsewhere in the congested beachhead area was inevitable. These are two of five vehicles hit by German bombs during a daylight raid on 7 February.*

THE BUTTERFLY BOMB. *When this German anti-personnel weapon is dropped, it falls a distance and the case is blown open, releasing a number of small delayed-action bombs which, before exploding, often lie on the ground for a day or two. Photo taken in the Peter Beach area on 15 February 1944.*

Along the front, 7 February was a quiet day; in the rear, bombing raids covered the port area with high explosives and antipersonnel bombs. At 0810 twenty Focke-Wulf 190's and Messerschmitt 109's dove out of the sun to attack Anzio and Nettuno. Bombs landing near VI Corps headquarters at Nettuno blew up three ammunition trucks, destroyed a number of buildings, and caused heavy casualties. At 1135 fifteen Focke-Wulf 190's and Messerschmitt 109's bombed and strafed the harbor area. An LCI and an LCT were damaged, thirty men were killed, and forty were wounded. At 1525 the enemy fighter-bombers were over again. One plane, under attack by a British Spit-fire, jettisoned its load of antipersonnel bombs in an effort to gain altitude. The bombs fell in the area of the 95th Evacuation Hospital, riddling the administration and operating tents. Chief Nurse 1st Lt. Blanche F. Sigman and two other nurses were standing by the bedside of a patient to whom they had just given blood plasma. All three were killed. A litter bearer carrying a patient into an operating tent sacrificed his life when he shielded the wounded soldier with his own body. In all, twenty-eight hospital personnel and patients were killed and sixty-four wounded, including the commanding officer. X-ray and surgical equipment was damaged. Medical installations continued to be bombed and shelled throughout the period of the beachhead; the hospital area came to be known to front-line troops as "Hell's Half Acre." It is doubtful, aside from the sinking of the hospital ship H.M.S. *David* on 24 January, that the enemy deliberately bombed or shelled medical installations. It was impossible to locate the hospitals in areas completely apart from military installations, and they were never more than six to eight miles from the front lines. During the rainy winter season, also, the ground was too wet to permit the tents to be dug in deeply. There were no safe areas at Anzio. Nurses and quartermaster depot men, as well as the men in the front lines, were subject to shelling and bombing. Nevertheless, the enemy paid dearly for the air attacks. On 7 February anti-aircraft guns accounted for 7 planes destroyed, 6 probables, and 9 damaged; defending fighters destroyed 17 with 12 probables.

## The Factory and Carroceto

The swift and thorough measures of VI Corps to prepare a strongly organized and coordinated system of defenses were based on the certain knowledge that the enemy would resume the offensive as soon as he had grouped his forces. On the night of 6 February orders were sent out to all front-line units to be alert for a possible attack the next morning. Intelligence sources in Rome had reported that the enemy was planning a major

attack to be launched at 0400, 7 February. It was anticipated that the attack would be directed against the 3d Division, and General Clark arranged for strong air support to be ready on call, with strategic bombers prepared to attack Cisterna and Velletri. The expected offensive failed to develop at the reported time. Just before midnight on 6 February the enemy laid down a concentration of 800 rounds of medium artillery fire on the positions of the 2d Battalion, 157th Infantry, along the Moletta River line. At 2400 an enemy force of approximately one company launched an attack. By 0110 the enemy had been thrown back with heavy losses, and there was no further action during the night. Indications of the impending offensive, how-

ever, continued to accumulate during 7 February. There was an increase in artillery fire on the 1 Division front, the Factory (Aprilia) area was bombed and strafed, and prisoners were picked up who had deserted to avoid participation in the attack. The evidence pointed to a resumption of the enemy's drive in the British sector with the Factory area as the first objective. (Map No. 11.)

Capture of the Factory was the next logical move if the enemy planned to make his all-out effort along the axis of the Albano road. The Factory itself, before it was leveled by weeks of bombing and shelling, was a compact, geometrically laid out cluster of three- and four-story brick buildings designed in 1936 to be a model for Fascist

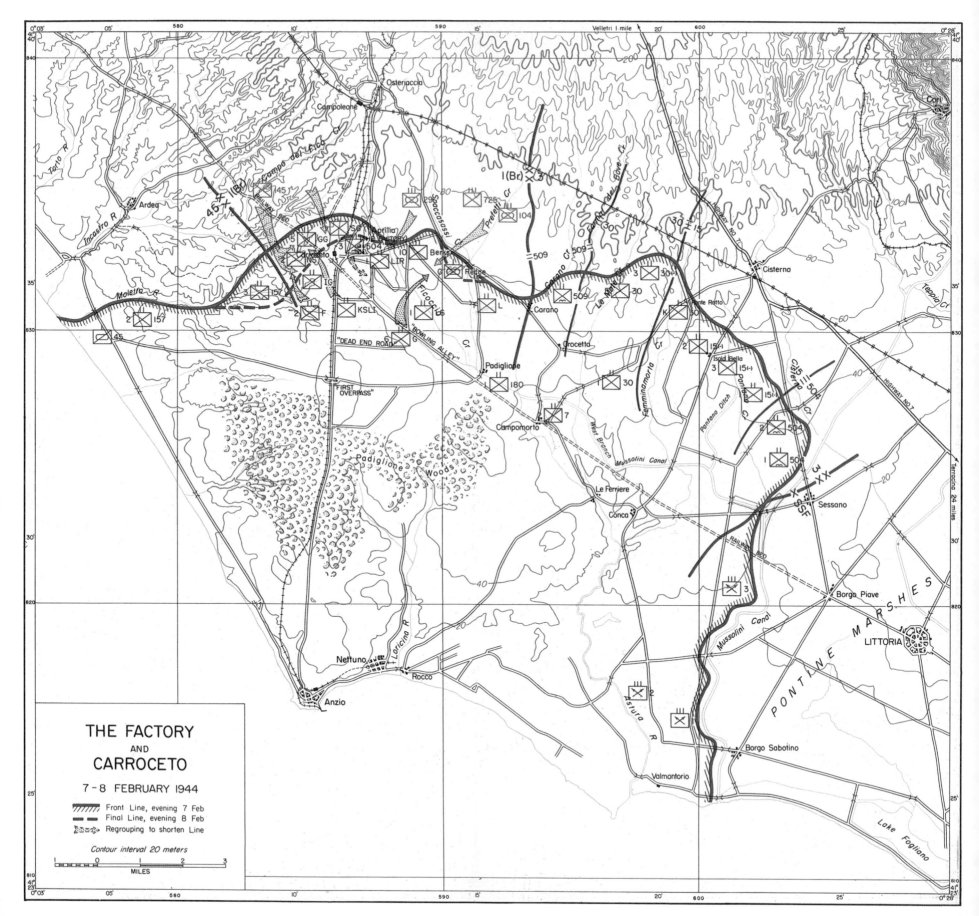

THE FACTORY
AND
CARROCETO

7-8 FEBRUARY 1944

///// Front Line, evening 7 Feb
▬ ▬ Final Line, evening 8 Feb
▶▶▶ Regrouping to shorten Line

Contour interval 20 meters

MILES

farm settlements. Located on a slight rise of ground, it stood like a fortress dominating the surrounding countryside. The hamlet of Carroceto, located 500 yards to the southwest of the Factory and just north of the overpass which crosses the Albano road and the parallel railway, was an equally important objective. Possession of the Factory and Carroceto would offer the enemy strong defensive positions as well as assembly areas from which to launch further attacks, for they were the focal points of a network of roads leading south and southeast. As the wet boggy ground of the beachhead made employment of tanks off the roads virtually impossible, control of the road network was of great tactical value to the attacker. Once the enemy had won the Factory and Carroceto, he would be in position to strike at several different points along the final beachhead line of defense.

To protect the Factory area the 1 Division had three brigades in the forward line. West of the Albano road the 24 Guards Brigade held Buonriposo Ridge with the 2 North Staffs, the 5 Grenadier Guards, and the 1 Scots Guards. The center was held by the 168 Brigade with the 3d Battalion, 504th Parachute Infantry, astride the Albano road and the 1 London Irish Rifles and the 10 Battalion, Royal Berkshire Regiment, along the lateral road leading east from the Factory. The 2 Brigade held the right flank with a squadron of the 1 Recce Regiment and the 1 Loyals. Division reserve consisted of the whole of the 3 Brigade. After the losses sustained in the fighting at Campoleone the 1 Division was considerably below strength, and the troops, fighting in rain, mud, and near-freezing weather, had had little rest since D Day.

The enemy plan of attack called for a simultaneous assault on the night of 7–8 February by the *65th Infantry Division* from the west, and by *Combat Group Graeser* from the east, converging

on Carroceto and the Factory. The attack started at 2100, 7 February, with heavy artillery concentrations on both flanks of the 1 Division front. At 2115 the 3d Battalion, 157th Infantry, which was in contact with the 24 Guards Brigade along Buonriposo Ridge, reported its right flank under attack. The brunt of the blow, however, was borne by the adjoining 2 North Staffs. Infiltrating rapidly and in small groups, the *145th Infantry Regiment (65th Infantry Division)* crossed the Moletta River and fought its way east toward the Albano road. Before midnight the attack had spread along the whole front of the 24 Guards Brigade. With the advantage of a dark night and the numerous deep gullies which cut up the rough country west of the Albano road, the *65th Infantry Division* pushed deep into the positions of the British troops. The fighting along Buonriposo Ridge resolved itself into a series of confused hand-to-hand encounters as the strong points of the 2 North Staffs were isolated and overrun. In the early morning hours the 3d Battalion, 157th Infantry, discovered enemy tanks and infantry operating to its rear. At 0400 seventy men, all that was left of the company of the 2 North Staffs to its right, requested permission to attach themselves to the 3d Battalion; the British troops had used up all their ammunition and had to abandon their automatic weapons. In order to protect its right flank the 3d Battalion was ordered to withdraw to the stream line south of the ridge, and a company of the 179th Infantry was sent up to support it. By 0130 the reserve company of the 5 Grenadier Guards to the southwest of Carroceto was under pressure from German units attacking northeast along the Buonriposo Ridge line from the former positions of the 2 North Staffs, and the forward companies of the 5 Grenadier Guards and the 1 Scots Guards were under constant pressure from the north and west.

Small enemy units penetrated all the way to the main road before being wiped out. Fighting continued all morning as the *65th Infantry Division,* having achieved its first objective of seizing Buonriposo Ridge, sought to continue its advance toward Carroceto and the Factory.

The attack of *Combat Group Graeser* on the British right flank started more slowly. Shortly after 2200, 7 February, two companies attacked C Squadron, 1 Recce Regiment, and the right flank company of the 10 Royal Berks near the crossroads where the lateral road from the Factory meets the road to Carano. This force appeared to be covering a mine-lifting party. An hour later it had withdrawn under cover of a mortar barrage. By midnight both forward companies of the 1 London Irish were under pressure, and one platoon was overrun. The attack, launched by the *29th Panzer Grenadier Regiment (3d Panzer Grenadier Division)* followed the same tactics of rapid infiltration which were proving so successful on the west flank. Small groups armed with machine pistols and light machine guns would infiltrate behind the forward British units, cut communications, and organize

THE FACTORY, *focal point of the fighting on the beachhead right flank, was situated at the junction of a road network over which armor would be forced to operate in the area. The lateral road behind the Factory, the old railroad bed, and the first overpass north of Anzio became successive lines of battle as the fight went on.*

NETTUNO   ANZIO   FIRST OVERPASS   HIGHWAY

OLD RAILROAD BED

LATERAL ROAD

small pockets of resistance deep within the lines. After the defending troops had exhausted their ammunition firing on an enemy who appeared to be striking from all directions, the main enemy force would overrun the position. The *29th Panzer Grenadier Regiment* had only limited success with these tactics. This regiment had advanced too slowly, and accordingly all three battalions of the *725th Infantry Regiment (715th Infantry Division)* had to be committed. This attack also failed to make more than slight gains. One small group of the enemy got as far as the rear of the Factory, where the 894th Tank Destroyer Battalion had three tank destroyers. 1st Lt. Bernard T. Schaefer, moving his destroyer into position to fire on a house occupied by the enemy, killed forty with his .50-caliber machine gun while he blasted the building with his 3-inch gun. The remainder of the enemy force—thirty in all—surrendered. Other groups were held at the lateral road. A company of the 1 London Scottish was sent up to plug a gap between the 1 London Irish and the 10 Royal Berks, and a local counterattack supported by three tanks drove back the enemy unit which had captured a bridge on the lateral road just to the east of the Factory. The only important success won by *Combat Group Graeser* was on the right flank near the crossroads. Attacking at dawn on 8 February, a battalion of the *104th Panzer Grenadier Regiment* overran C Squadron, 1 Recce Regiment, and a platoon of the 6 Gordons which was supporting it. The Germans then dug in with two companies on each side of the road between the positions of the 10 Royal Berks and the 1 Loyals. Employing small groups of tanks in support of the infantry, the enemy kept up the pressure on the 168 Brigade all day without succeeding in gaining control of the important lateral road.

General Penney decided to deal first with the critical situation on the left flank. Orders were issued to the 3d Battalion, 504th Parachute Infantry, to move south of Carroceto where it could be employed as a counterattack force to support the 24 Guards Brigade. Its former positions north of the overpass were filled by the 1 Scots Guards.

At 1400 General Penney committed his divisional reserve, the 3 Brigade, to regain the positions of the 2 North Staffs along Buonriposo Ridge. The 3 Brigade employed two battalions, the 2 Foresters and the 1 KSLI, attacking abreast with armored support by a squadron of the 46 Royal Tanks and a platoon of Company C, 894th Tank Destroyer Battalion. The 2 Foresters made good progress in clearing the lower end of the ridge; the 1 KSLI was held up on the upper end by machine-gun fire. The Germans had dug in well, and both battalions suffered heavy casualties during the attack. In the meantime Lt. Col. Leslie G. Freeman, commander of the 3d Battalion, 504th Parachute Infantry, was moving his battalion to positions south of Carroceto. The paratroopers of Company H were committed that night to assist the 5 Grenadier Guards west of the overpass. Although the counterattacks succeeded in retaking only a portion of the lost ground, they served to bolster the hard-pressed 24 Guards Brigade.

The enemy devoted the remainder of the afternoon to digging in and consolidating his positions along Buonriposo Ridge, while the 1 Division reorganized its forces. After the counterattack launched by the 3 Brigade, the 1 KSLI and the 2 Foresters were left in position to strengthen the left flank. On the right the 6 Gordons was moved up from 2 Brigade reserve to help fill the gap between the 10 Royal Berks and the 1 Loyals. To strengthen the 6 Gordons, which had been reduced to two companies during the battle for the Campoleone salient, the 238 Field Company, Royal Engineers, and a company made up from 3 Beach Group personnel were added. The commitment of the 6 Gordons was balanced by moving the 1st Battalion, 180th Infantry, to previously prepared positions near Padiglione where it could be employed either as a reserve or counterattack force. Of the 2 North Staffs only 17 officers and 364 men were left at the end of the day. These were reorganized by their commanding officer into a rifle company. The 1 Division had been seriously weakened, but it had succeeded in checking the enemy's initial assault.

NO MAN'S LAND *on the right flank along the Mussolini Canal gave the appearance during daylight of being deserted, as troops of both forces stayed in their foxholes. In this photo the road in the foreground is the Allies' front line, the enemy being some distance beyond the point of the smoke burst.*

Ground action on the remainder of the VI Corps front was confined to small-scale company actions and patrolling. On the night of 7–8 February Company E, 15th Infantry, attacked north up the road paralleling Femminamorta Creek with the objective of capturing the farm east of Ponte Rotto; Company F, 30th Infantry, attacked from the west to secure the road junction just beyond Ponte Rotto bridge. Both attacks achieved limited results. At 2100 enemy tanks and infantry pushed down the road from Cisterna toward Isola Bella. Tank fire collapsed some buildings in which Company G, 15th Infantry, had organized positions. After losing some ground Company G fought its way back

before daylight. A second company-strength attack, supported by tanks, struck Company G, 30th Infantry. It was beaten back.

On 8 February, while heavy fighting was in progress on the 1 Division front, only one attack, a raid aimed at the village of Carano, struck the 3d Division. In beating off the attack the 509th Parachute Infantry Battalion captured ten prisoners and killed twenty-five of the enemy, most of whom were from the *114th Light Division.*

Activity on the right flank of the beachhead was carried on by the 1st Special Service Force under Brig. Gen. Robert T. Frederick. On the night of 2–3 February, when the unit took over the right flank of the beachhead, the enemy outpost line was along the Mussolini Canal. After a week of aggressive patrolling, the enemy had been forced back 1,500 yards, leaving a broad no man's land between the opposing forces. During the day this area appeared to be a peaceful expanse of level farmland; at night the 1st Special Service Force kept it alive with hard-hitting patrols which gave the enemy no rest. Although the right flank of the beachhead with its soft ground and numerous drainage ditches was not favorable terrain for a major attack, the 1st Special Service Force never permitted it to remain a quiet sector of the front. During the night of 8–9 February the 2d Com-

pany, 2d Regiment, staged a successful raid on the village of Sessano. The German company which was holding Sessano was almost annihilated. After taking 7 prisoners, killing at least 40 of the enemy, and holding the village for 3 hours, the Special Service troops withdrew. Accurate artillery fire adjusted on a reserve company organizing for a counterattack cost the enemy an additional 20 dead, and the rear guard of the assault company accounted for 20 more. The 2d Company itself suffered only 15 casualties.

During 8 February VI Corps artillery, in addition to supporting the fire of the 1 Division guns, executed a coordinated program of counterbattery

COUNTERBATTERY FIRE BY ANTIAIRCRAFT UNITS *was added to the coordinated program of VI Corps artillery against known German positions and troop concentrations. Here the 68th Coast Artillery (AA) lowers the muzzle of a 90-mm. rifle to add to the barrage.*

fire on all known enemy gun positions on the west flank of the beachhead. In response to an emergency request, two British cruisers, the *Orion* and *Phoebe,* and one American cruiser, the *Brooklyn,* moved up from Naples to add the fires of their 5-inch and 6-inch guns. Good weather permitted accurate air spotting by the 111th Reconnaissance Squadron. Fighter-bombers of the XII Air Support Command and guns of the 68th Coast Artillery Regiment (Antiaircraft), the 1st Armored and 45th Divisions, and the 976th Field Artillery Battalion, all joined in blasting the enemy gun positions and assembly areas. Dive-bombers also gave close support to the ground troops. They dropped smoke bombs and high explosives and strafed enemy troops, while forty-eight B–25 mediums bombed Cisterna.

Following the same pattern of attack he had employed the previous day, the enemy renewed his efforts to take the Factory area during the early morning hours of 9 February. (Map No. 12.) Shortly after midnight, following a heavy concentration of mortar and artillery fire, enemy units began infiltrating at various points all along the 1 Division front. On the western flank, where the 5 Grenadier Guards and the 1 Scots Guards were protecting Carroceto, elements of the *65th Infantry Division* forced the 5 Grenadier Guards back to the railroad station and overpass. There they held. At the same time the enemy units dug in along Buonriposo Ridge drove south against the 1 KSLI and the 2 Foresters, pushing them back from their newly won positions to the stream line south of the ridge.

The main attack was launched by *Combat Group Graeser* against the 168 Brigade, covering the Factory and the lateral road to the east. For the attack Maj. Gen. Fritz H. Graeser threw in his remaining reserve, the *735th Infantry Regiment,* to reinforce the *725th Infantry Regiment* and the *29th* and *104th Panzer Grenadier Regiments,* which had been committed the previous day. During the night, small units penetrated at several points along the lateral road and in the Factory area. At daylight the major force, supported by

a few tanks, drove through to capitalize on the gains made by the infiltrating groups. The fighting spread along the whole front of the 168 Brigade. To the east of the Factory, between the 1 London Irish and the 10 Royal Berks, elements of the *29th Panzer Grenadier Regiment* pushed south as much as 2,000 yards. Farther to the east the *104th Panzer Grenadier Regiment* overran the right flank company of the 10 Royal Berks, clearing the way for enemy tanks and self-propelled guns to use the lateral road. Exploiting these gains, the *735th Infantry Regiment* fought its way into the Factory. By early afternoon the enemy controlled both the lateral road and the Factory. He lost no time in bringing up antitank guns and consolidating his gains. On the left the hard-pressed 5 Grenadier Guards and the 1 Scots Guards, aided by a counterattack launched at 0630 by the 3d Battalion, 504th Parachute Infantry, held stubbornly to their positions covering Carroceto.

To give the 1 Division support against the enemy penetrations the 1st Armored Division employed two companies of medium and two companies of light tanks in counterattacks. At 0900, 9 February, General Harmon ordered Major Tuck to alert his 1st Battalion, 1st Armored Regiment, to attack Buonriposo Ridge with light tanks. Company A moved up the Albano road to the first overpass, turned west on the lateral road which formed part of the final beachhead line of defense, and then swung north along a dirt road. Under artillery and antitank fire it made slow progress once it left the highway, and at the end of the morning it was only a mile north of the overpass. The tanks knocked out one Mark IV and assisted in breaking up the attack of an estimated battalion of infantry. At noon, Company B was ordered forward to attack the south side of the ridge. Following a dirt trail, it moved up to the stream line in the positions of the 1 KSLI and 2 Foresters. Here it encountered a hasty mine field, which caused the loss of two tanks; the company commander, 1st Lt. William W. Beckett, was wounded. The company attempted to get around the field and push on. As soon as the tanks left the road

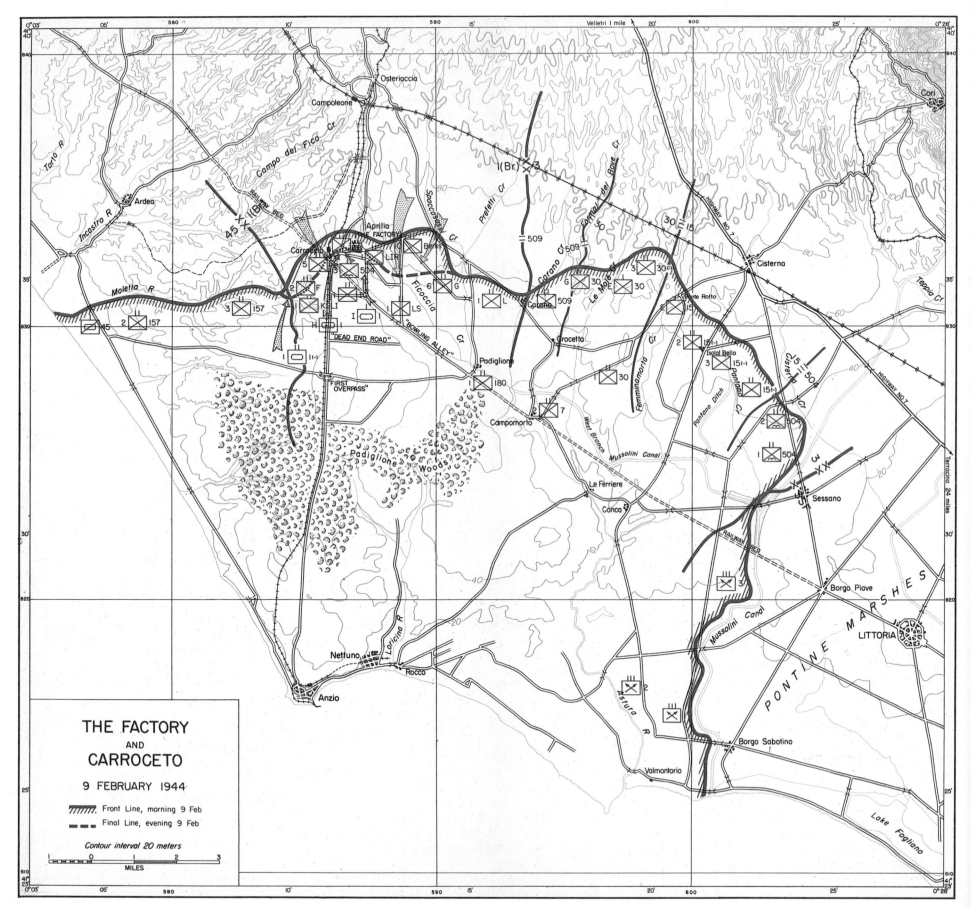

THE FACTORY
AND
CARROCETO

9 FEBRUARY 1944

⑅⑅⑅⑅ Front Line, morning 9 Feb
▬ ▬ ▬ Final Line, evening 9 Feb

Contour interval 20 meters

0    1    2    3
MILES

they sank into deep mud and five tanks became mired. Accurate antitank fire and intense small-arms fire forced the company to withdraw with a loss of seven tanks.

At noon the 3d Battalion, 1st Armored Regiment, was ordered to send one company of medium tanks up the Albano road to the Factory and a second company to the right of the Factory. Company H followed the main road to a point beyond the Factory where it was stopped by a mine field which the German engineers had laid across the road. The Factory itself was bristling with antitank guns. In the area of the 5 Grenadier Guards, Company H knocked out one tank and two antitank guns, and helped drive back two battalions of infantry; north of the Factory it destroyed two Mark IV tanks before withdrawing late in the afternoon. On the right, Company I followed the "bowling alley," a road leading northwest from Padiglione to the overpass below the Factory, and then turned north behind the 1 London Irish. Roadbound and under antitank-gun fire it was able to give the 1 London Irish only limited help in mopping up the enemy penetration east of the Factory.

Continuing the program of the previous day, VI Corps artillery on 9 February carried out another coordinated air, artillery, and naval counterbattery shoot on the left flank of the beachhead. The British destroyer *Loyal* while laying a smoke screen for the cruisers was hit and slightly damaged by a shell from a German shore battery. It had to be sent back to Naples for repairs. Trouble was also experienced in obtaining air observation. A wind of near-gale proportions held the P–51 observation planes on the ground and prevented all unloading from Liberty ships in the harbor. A cub plane from the 976th Field Artillery Battalion managed to get off the ground during the afternoon and so enabled the cruisers to do some observed firing. In the morning Fifth Army had requested that as much air support as possible be given to VI Corps. One hundred and four fighter-bombers, thirty-six light bombers, and eighty-four medium bombers were sent up. Medium bombers, briefed to bomb supply dumps between Valmontone and Palestrina,

switched to assembly areas around Campoleone with excellent results. A more extensive program was prepared for the next day.

Late in the afternoon on 9 February the fighting slackened. Both enemy and Allied units had suffered heavy losses; both sides were near the point of exhaustion. The enemy seized the opportunity to consolidate his positions while the 1 Division reorganized. To relieve some of the pressure on the seriously depleted British force, the 180th Infantry took over the positions of the 2 Brigade, which then passed into division reserve along the final beachhead line. This left the 1 Division three brigades with which to cover its reduced front. The 168 Brigade held the right flank east and south of the Factory, which was now firmly in enemy hands; the 24 Guards Brigade covered Carroceto, with the 1 Scots Guards still holding a narrow salient north of the village astride the railroad; and the 3 Brigade held the left sector along the ravine south of Buonriposo Ridge. The battered, tired troops worked feverishly through the night to wire in their positions and prepare for new attacks. General Brann, Army G–3, reported that the 1 Division was at not over 50 percent effective strength, and he concurred with General Lucas that another division was needed to hold the beachhead until main Fifth Army could break through the Gustav Line on the southern front.

By early afternoon on 9 February, after twelve hours of heavy fighting, *Combat Group Graeser* had achieved the German's main objective, the capture of the Factory. (Map No. 13.) The 1 Division still held Carroceto and the overpass. Taking advantage of the observation provided by the Factory buildings, the enemy directed fire all afternoon on the 1 Scots Guards, the 5 Grenadier Guards, and the 3d Battalion, 504th Parachute Infantry. Shortly after midnight approximately fifteen enemy tanks emerged from the Factory and together with a battalion of infantry struck the 1 Scots Guards. Tank destroyers of Company B, 894th Tank Destroyer Battalion, and artillery fire broke up the armored attack and the infantry was driven off. At 0430, 10 February, the 5 Grenadier Guards and the paratroopers were under attack from three sides. With the help of a squadron of the 46 Royal Tank Regiment they held out. North of Carroceto the situation of the 1 Scots Guards gradually deteriorated during the bitter-cold, moonlit night. All contact was lost with the two forward companies, and the remainder of the battalion, in danger of being cut off, withdrew within the perimeter defense of the 5 Grenadier Guards protecting the overpass. Company B's tank destroyers, acting as a rearguard, covered the withdrawal with their .50-caliber machine guns. The "fighting tank busters," as the British troops called them, appeared to be all over the battlefield. In addition to their normal role, they operated as tanks, as mobile pillboxes, as assault artillery, and even as infantry. The British troops, fighting against odds, needed their support. At 0530 General Penney reported that his troops had been fighting all night, and that the division could not continue to hold out without the support of a counterattack by fresh troops prepared to take over the major part of the 1 Division front.

Corps artillery and the Air Force gave all the aid they could muster to support the hard-pressed division. At 0900 two enemy attacks forming near the Carroceto railway station were broken up by a concentration of 200 guns representing both division and Corps artillery. At the same time, wave after wave of heavy, medium, and light bombers dropped their bombs on assembly areas along the Albano road from Campoleone to Albano. All the available resources of the Strategical, Tactical, and Desert Air Forces and XII Air Support Command were allotted to VI Corps. Unfortunately a heavy overcast began developing at 0945 and an hour later further bombing was out of the question, Many of the medium and heavy bombers were forced to turn back without unloading their bombs.

The *65th Infantry Division,* attacking from the west, occupied Carroceto station during the morning of 10 February. An Allied counterattack during the day, supported by tanks, recaptured the station. But it was retaken in the evening by *Combat Group Graeser,* striking from the east.

With the capture of the Factory and Carroceto, the German *Fourteenth Army* had won its initial objectives after three days of bitter fighting. Each day the Germans were forced to throw in more and more of their reserves until they had committed the equivalent of over six full regiments. Their tactics of night infiltration had proved very successful; but during the daylight hours, when Allied artillery could fire on observed targets, their troops suffered disproportionately heavy losses. Air bombardment and naval gunfire also aided in disorganizing the enemy attacks. The Germans had to pause to consolidate their gains and bring up additional fresh troops before renewing their offensive.

## Allied Counterattacks

The hard and protracted struggle to hold the Factory area had drained the fighting strength of the 1 Division. It was in no condition to launch a counterattack or even to hold the positions to which it had been forced back. On the afternoon of 10 February the 168 Brigade was estimated to be at less than one-third normal strength, and many other units were at no better than half-strength. In addition, the weather for the past three days had been cold, windy, and rainy. Fox holes dug in the wet, boggy ground quickly filled with water, and after a few days in the line troops suffered from trench foot and exposure. It was important for VI Corps not only to regain the Factory area but also to effect the relief of at least a major part of the 1 Division. The first step had been taken on the night of 9–10 February when the 180th Infantry under Col. Robert L. Dulaney took over the positions of the 2 Brigade on the right flank of the division. The next night the 179th Infantry under Col. Malcolm R. Kammerer relieved the 168 Brigade with the 3d Battalion and prepared to launch a counterattack on the morning of 11 February to retake the Factory with the 1st Battalion.

The commitment of two regiments of the 45th Division in the 1 Division sector resulted in a depletion of VI Corps reserves. To offset this loss the 36th Engineer Combat Regiment took over a por-

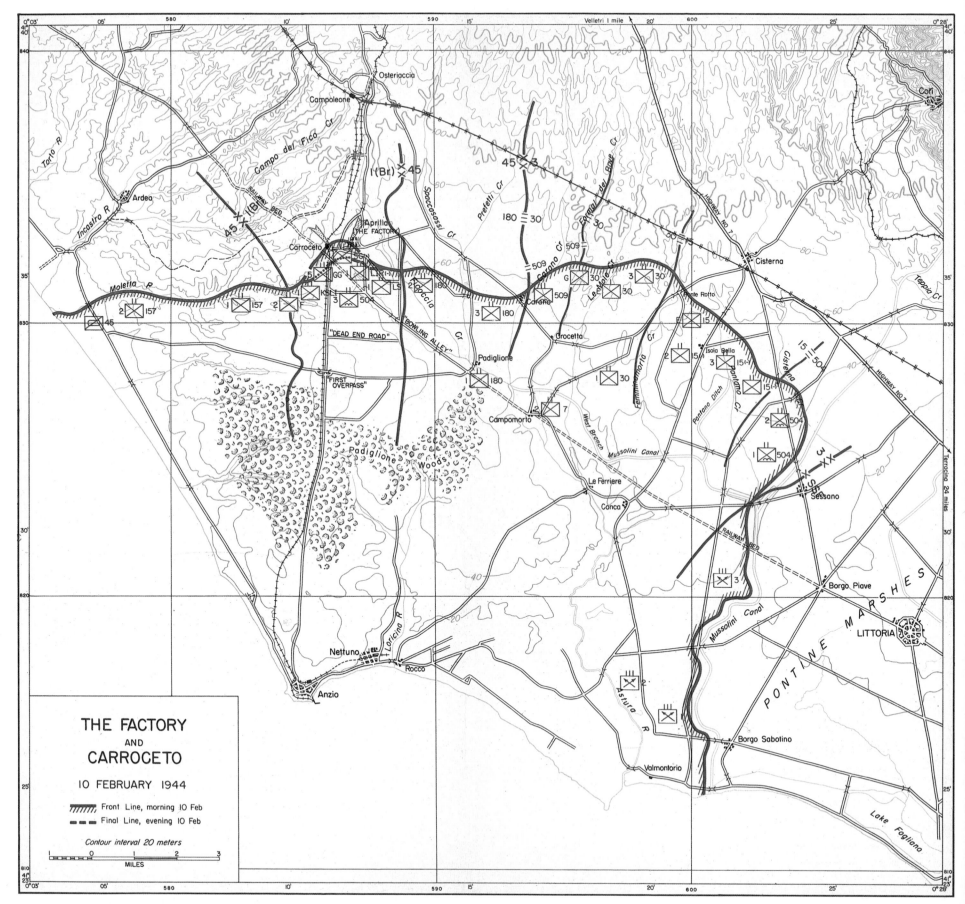

THE FACTORY
AND
CARROCETO

10 FEBRUARY 1944

Front Line, morning 10 Feb
Final Line, evening 10 Feb

Contour interval 20 meters

MILES

MAP NO. 13

tion of the Moletta River line, relieving all but one battalion of the 157th Infantry. Although the engineers had had no experience as infantry and were badly needed for construction of defenses and road maintenance, by holding a relatively quiet portion of the front they released infantry troops needed to bolster the critical central sector. In the succeeding weeks while the regiment continued to maintain the Moletta River line the engineers were to prove themselves able to handle machine guns and mortars as capably as they handled bulldozers and road graders.

The reliefs carried out by the 45th Division left the 1 Division holding less than half of its former front. It was then possible to move all of the 168 Brigade to a rear bivouac area for rest and reorganization. Responsibility for the newly defined division sector passed to the 3 Brigade, reinforced by the 3d Battalion, 504th Parachute Infantry Regiment, the 1 Irish Guards, and the 1 Recce Regiment, less one squadron. The new front extended from the positions of the 2 Foresters and the 1 KSLI south of Buonriposo Ridge to a point just east of the Albano road where the 1 DWR relieved

**THE OVERPASS AT CARROCETO,** *scarred by both Allied and enemy fire, was the jump-off point for armor attacking toward the Factory on 11 February. This photo, taken a year after the action, shows the rubble heap that was Carroceto. The overpass carried the old railroad bed over the Anzio–Albano road.*

GERMAN ARTILLERY IN THE FACTORY *was in a well-concealed position to hamper Allied armor attacking the position. In the foreground is a modified German 150-mm. infantry howitzer, and behind it a knocked-out American Sherman tank and an enemy medium armored personnel carrier. The photo was transmitted to America during World War II by news sources in a neutral country.*

the 1 Scots Guards and the 5 Grenadier Guards, which had been covering the overpass below Carroceto. Back along the final beachhead line the 2 Brigade was engaged in fortification. (Map No. 14.)

For the counterattack to regain the Factory, Maj. Gen. William W. Eagles, commanding the 45th Division, committed the 1st Battalion, 179th Infantry, and two companies of the attached 191st Tank Battalion. One tank company was to attack through the overpass at Carroceto to strike the Factory from the west; the other company was to move up the north–south road just east of the Factory to

strike it from the southeast. The infantry were to coordinate their advance with the tanks. On 11 February at 0630, following a 15-minute artillery concentration on the Factory, the tanks and infantry jumped off. Company A, 191st Tank Battalion, drove up the Albano road. The first tank to pass through the overpass was knocked out by a direct hit; a second tank blew up 200 yards farther along the road. At 0830, after shelling the southwest corner of the Factory, the tanks of Company A withdrew under a smoke screen. Company A, 179th Infantry, attacking behind the protective fire of the

64

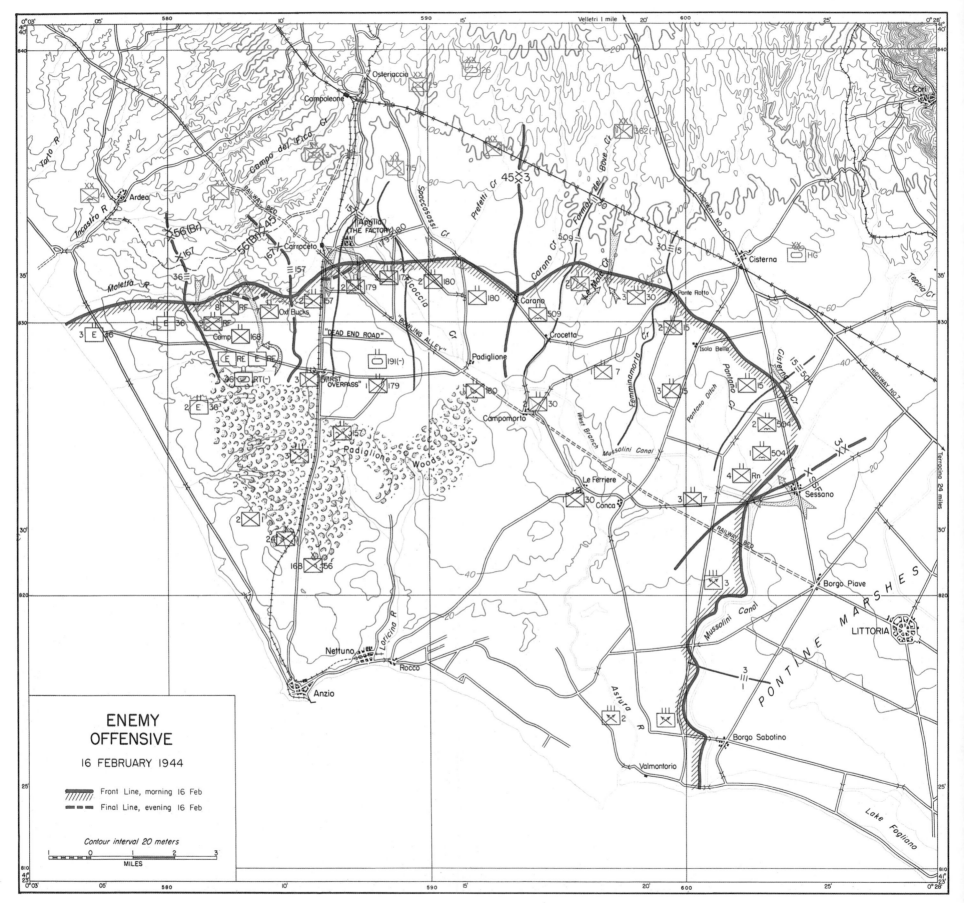

ENEMY
OFFENSIVE

16 FEBRUARY 1944

▨▨▨▨ Front Line, morning 16 Feb

▬ ▬ ▬ Final Line, evening 16 Feb

Contour interval 20 meters

MILES
0    1    2    3

MAP NO. 15

# THE MAJOR GERMAN OFFENSIVE (16-20 February)

The capture of the Factory, Carroceto, and Buonriposo Ridge to the west provided the Germans with the key positions from which they could launch their all-out attack on the Anzio beachhead. The network of roads leading south and southeast offered the opportunity for the employment of tanks; no natural obstacles would impede the advance. Once the enemy crossed the three miles of open country lying between the Factory area and the final beachhead defense line, he could employ his favorite tactics of infiltration; the tangled underbrush and scrub forest of the Padiglione Woods stretched southward from the final beachhead line almost to Anzio. Allied air reconnaissance disclosed to VI Corps the regrouping of enemy forces, the forward movement of field artillery, and the movement of heavy traffic on the railroads and roads leading from the area of Rome to the beachhead. The Allied command assumed that as soon as the Germans had completed the regrouping of their forces they would attack down the Albano road, and at the same time launch diversionary attacks along the whole Anzio front.

## Preparing for the Attack

*Fourteenth Army* issued its preliminary order for the major German offensive on 9 February. The main effort was to be made along a 4-mile front astride the Anzio–Albano road, from Buonriposo Ridge on the west to Spaccasassi Creek on the east. After piercing the main beachhead defense line, the Germans planned to drive through to Anzio and Nettuno, splitting VI Corps and destroying its separated parts. The assault was to be commanded by *I Parachute Corps* to the west of the Anzio road, and by *LXXVI Panzer Corps* to the east. (Map No. 15.) The first wave of the assault was to include six divisions—the *4th Parachute* (elements only) and *65th Infantry Divisions* under *I Parachute Corps,* and the *3d Panzer Grenadier, 114th Light Infantry, 715th Infantry,* and *Hermann Goering Panzer* (elements only) *Divisions* under *LXXVI Panzer Corps*—supported by a variety of miscellaneous units. The *26th Panzer* and *29th Panzer Grenadier Divisions,* and two battalions of Panther and Tiger tanks, were to be held in reserve, and thrown into the battle as soon as the first assault wave had pierced the main Allied defenses. This was a formidable force. *Fourteenth Army* on 12 February had at least 120,000 troops—including 70,000 combat troops—under its command. Although this number included forces guarding Rome and the coastal sector north of Anzio, the great bulk of the enemy troops were massed around the Anzio beachhead perimeter. The preliminary order of 9 February provided that the attack should be launched at H Hour on 15 February; subsequently (13 February), the time was fixed at 0630, 16 February. Essentially, the enemy tactical scheme was to break

OSTERIACCIA

CAMPOLEONE
STATION

CAMPOLEONE - CISTERNA
RAILROAD

ROAD BED

FACTORY

CARROCETO
OVERPASS

BUONRIPOSO
RIDGE

FICOCCIA CREEK

MOLETTA RIVER

SPACCASASSI CREEK

CARROCETO CREEK

"THE CAVES"
AREA

HIGHWAY AND RAILROAD
TO ANZIO

"THE BOWLING ALLEY"

DEAD END ROAD

FIRST
OVERPASS

PADIGLIONE

LATERAL ROAD

the main Allied defense line by massed infantry attacks backed by tanks, and then to follow through with the armored reserve.

The enemy planned to hold the remainder of the beachhead perimeter with the bare minimum of forces during its all-out assault along the Albano road. To deceive the Allies, the Germans assembled their armored reserve behind Cisterna on the U.S. 3d Division front, and planned to move it at the latest possible moment to the rear of the initial assault forces. Actually, by 12 February, the Germans realized that VI Corps was well informed (through aerial observation) about German movements and intentions; they also concluded that the Allies had given up any immediate intention of returning to the offensive themselves, and that they were concentrating on digging in to prepare for the German drive.

General Mackensen seems to have entertained some doubt about the ability of his *Fourteenth Army* to push through to the sea and eliminate the Anzio beachhead, but the German High Command appears to have viewed the prospect with optimism. Hitler gave his personal approval to the plan of attack on 11 February. For success, the Germans counted on their superiority in numbers and in some forms of equipment. They had a greater number of heavy artillery weapons than VI Corps, and a more adequate supply of ammunition than they possessed on other fronts at this time. But the enemy did not underestimate the Allies' capacity to resist their assault. VI Corps had superior air support, and its artillery could be supplemented by naval gunfire. Despite Allied logistical difficulties, the Germans realized that VI Corps' ammunition supply, and therefore its artillery fire, would be superior to any which they could themselves deliver in support of their massed infantry attack. Enemy intelligence noted that, while Allied units, especially the British 1 Division and U.S. 3d Division, had suffered heavy losses, the morale of VI Corps

was good and the Allies could be expected to defend their positions stubbornly.

General Clark for some time had been aware of the necessity of reinforcing VI Corps if it was to hold the beachhead, and also maintain sufficient reserves to resume the offensive as soon as the force of the enemy counterattacks had been spent. As fast as shipping space could be made available, troops and equipment were rushed to Anzio. By clever use of camouflage the illusion was created that the British 56 Division was moving into a rest area behind the southern front. Actually it was on its way to the beachhead. The 168 Brigade had arrived on 3 February and had been committed to support the 1 Division. The remainder of the division landed over a period of several days, with the 167 Brigade coming in on 13 February and the 169 Brigade on 18 February.

The arrival of the 167 Brigade permitted VI Corps to complete the relief of the 1 Division, which then passed into Corps reserve. On the night of 14 February the 167 Brigade took over the short sector of the Moletta River line held by the 3d Battalion, 157th Infantry. The following night, on the eve of the German attack, the sector held by the 1 Division was divided between the 56 and the 45th Divisions. The left position was taken over by the 56 Division, giving it a unified front extending from the positions of the 36th Engineers along the Moletta River to the point of contact with the 45th Division west of the Albano road. All three battalions of the 167 Brigade were committed: the 9 Royal Fusiliers on the left, the 8 Royal Fusiliers in the center, and the 7 Oxfordshire and Buckinghamshire Light Infantry (7 Oxford Bucks) on the right. Two companies of Royal Engineers, fighting as infantry, were employed to bolster the line, and the 46 Royal Tanks and 1 Division artillery were left in support. The right portion of the former 1 Division sector was taken over by the 157th Infantry under Col. John H. Church. The 179th Infantry

THE ALBANO ROAD SECTOR *is shown in its entirety by this photomosaic compiled in February 1944. Approximate scale: 1:50.000.*

held the center, and the 180th Infantry the right flank of the 45th Division line. When the Germans attacked on the morning of 16 February General Lucas had reasonably fresh troops holding the whole of the critical portion of the beachhead defense line lying astride the Albano road.

Corps artillery was strengthened by the arrival of the 977th Field Artillery Battalion, and antiaircraft units were built up steadily to aid in combatting the enemy's raids on the harbor area. In air and medium and light artillery power VI Corps far surpassed the enemy. There were 432 artillery pieces on the Corps front, not including the weapons of the infantry cannon companies. The enemy had 452 guns available to support his attack, but his ammunition supply was far inferior to that of VI Corps. Even with limitations imposed on some types of ammunition, Allied artillery by 14 February was firing about 20,000 rounds per day, and Allied destroyers and cruisers thickened the artillery fire almost daily. The enemy artillery fire falling in the harbor and beachhead areas was estimated by the VI Corps fire control center at not more than 1,500 rounds daily before 16 February.

VI Corps took advantage of a period of good weather, 12–16 February, to request as much air support as possible against the enemy's heavy-caliber guns. Locating and knocking out the guns was a difficult task. The enemy was adept at camouflaging his positions; the railroad guns in particular were moved frequently. On 13 February P–40's scored hits at the entrance to the railroad tunnel near Lake Albano and on a bridge along the railroad from Campoleone to Rome. The next day two railroad guns near the bombed bridge were attacked by P–40's and shelled by VI Corps artillery, adjusted by P–51 observers. This was one of the more successful aerial attacks on enemy railroad guns, for one gun car was derailed and the other destroyed. Other bombers concentrated on the Rome railway yards, on traffic moving south from Rome, and on assembly areas near the beachhead.

The Germans also increased the tempo of their air effort and their artillery fire on the eve of the big attack. On 15 February there were eight air raids in the Anzio area; an LCT loaded with gasoline went up in flames and a Liberty ship was damaged. Heavy caliber shells whistled over the front lines toward the harbor where they threw up geysers of water or crashed into buildings, continuing the work of destroying the summer hotels and palatial villas along the water's edge. Defending antiaircraft guns filled the sky with high altitude 90-mm. shells and with a crisscross pattern of 40-mm. red tracer shells which shot up like balls of light from dozens of Roman candles.

During the night of 15–16 February, Allied troops in the forward beachhead defense lines listened for the sounds of field artillery and *nebelwerfer* fire which would warn them of the expected attack. Few shells came in and patrols and outposts reported little activity along the front. The relief of the 1 Division was completed without incident. Before dawn there was no visible evidence of the impending attack, but the very silence was ominous.

## *The First Day, 16 February*

On the morning of 16 February, at 0600, enemy guns opened up along the central beachhead front. For half an hour the forward areas were alive with bursting shells and a pall of smoke gradually spread over the battlefield. Partly concealed by the smoke, assault waves of gray-green uniformed troops swept forward to strike at points along the outpost line of the beachhead defenses.

The brunt of the enemy attack was borne by the U.S. 45th Division, which held a 6-mile sector of the front that coincided almost exactly with that upon which the Germans had determined to concentrate their assault. At approximately 0630 the troops of the *3d Panzer Grenadier* and *715th Infantry Divisions,* supported by tanks, pushed forward against the 157th Infantry and the 179th Infantry holding the left and center of the 45th Division front. (Map No. 15.)

The tactical importance of holding the Factory and the overpass at Carroceto became immediately apparent from the attacks launched against the 2d and 3d Battalions, 179th Infantry, located to the

BOMBARDMENT OF THE ANZIO AND NETTUNO AREAS *was stepped up as the enemy prepared for his big offensive. An air strike destroyed this Liberty ship (above) in Anzio harbor. Long-range shelling of Nettuno (below) continued the reduction of buildings along the water's edge.*

south and southeast of the Factory, and against the 2d Battalion, 157th Infantry, astride the Albano road. From the Factory buildings the enemy could easily observe the positions of the 179th Infantry, and both the Factory and Carroceto provided concealed assembly areas for enemy infantry and tanks. Taking advantage of the network of roads in the area, groups of from four to eight tanks would issue forth from the Factory to pour fire at point-blank range into the fox holes of American troops. When out of ammunition they would withdraw to the Factory, replenish their supply, and return to the attack. Enemy infantry, coordinating their movements with the tanks, worked down La Ficoccia Creek against the 3d Battalion, 179th Infantry, and down Carroceto Creek against the 2d Battalion.

During the morning all attacks on the 179th Infantry were beaten off with heavy losses to the enemy. 1st Lt. Donald E. Knowlton, observer for the 160th Field Artillery Battalion, had set up his radio in an oven next to a farmhouse southeast of the Factory. When the infantry outposts were forced back by enemy tanks and infantry attacking from the Factory, he refused to withdraw. While continuing to adjust the artillery fire he killed two of the enemy and possibly a third with his carbine before a slug from a machine pistol struck him in the head. Left for dead by his men he was captured by the enemy and then recaptured when the fire he had called down on his position forced the enemy to withdraw. The enemy seemed to pay no attention to casualties. As fast as one wave of the attackers was broken it was replaced by another. Companies F and G along the gully of Carroceto Creek were forced to pull back slightly and a platoon of Company L was sent forward to assist Company I in fighting its way out of an enemy encirclement. Company F, gathering together the remnants of its scattered force, reported that it was down to thirty men and that it had lost all its machine guns. Late in the afternoon the pressure on the 179th Infantry eased; the troops were given an opportunity to reorganize, and many of the men reported missing filtered back to their units.

One enemy unit, the *309th Panzer Grenadier Regiment* (also called *Infantry Lehr Regiment*), fell back in disorder, and without permission, from the 179th Infantry sector in the afternoon of 16 February. This was an infantry demonstration regiment that had been rushed from Germany, and attached on the eve of the attack to the *3d Panzer Grenadier Division*. Allied artillery fire produced heavy casualties among the troops of this regiment; after having lost a high percentage of their officers, the troops broke and fled. This incident helped to ease the pressure on the 179th Infantry and to rob the German assault of its momentum.

Enemy tanks, as well as infantry, suffered heavy losses during these attacks. At noon, the 160th Field Artillery Battalion massed the fire of 144 guns on a concentration of infantry near the Factory; at 1545, firing with observation by the 645th Tank Destroyer Battalion, it knocked out three tanks in the same area; and at 1725 it set fire to four tanks and damaged another near a water tower northeast of the Factory. When the attack started, Sgt. Charles W. Keyser, in charge of three tanks of Company A, 191st Tank Battalion, was located behind a farmhouse 600 yards from the Factory. His No. 2 tank was knocked out in the morning by an artillery shell. At noon, enemy infantry worked down the ditch beside the road to the farmhouse. Turning the turret of his No. 1 tank he fired a 75-mm. shell which grazed the house and exploded in the midst of the enemy. A second attempt to take the house was broken up with hand grenades. Two enemy tanks approached down the road. Concealed by the cloud of dust around the house Sergeant Keyser moved his No. 1 tank out, knocked out one enemy tank with three rounds, and with four rounds set the other on fire. Well-placed shells disposed of the crews as they attempted to escape. At 1430 No. 3 tank received a direct hit. Sergeant Keyser's radio, which he had been using to direct artillery fire, was damaged and he failed to receive the order from his platoon leader, 1st Lt. William E. Nangle, to withdraw. At 1615 six more enemy tanks appeared. Laying his own smoke screen the sergeant tried to make a run for it across

DUGOUTS ALONG THE MUSSOLINI CANAL *had been fairly well prepared in every defilade. From positions such as these the 1st Special Service Force was able to stem enemy attempts to breach the right flank.*

country. Three hundred yards from the house his tank was hit and his driver killed. Badly burned, Sergeant Keyser hid in a ditch until after dark when he got back to his battalion. Altogether, for the loss of seven tanks, the 191st Tank Battalion destroyed fifteen of the enemy's. Seven others were knocked out by antitank guns.

The artillery fire preceding the enemy attacks reached its greatest intensity along the front of the 2d Battalion, 157th Infantry, astride the Albano road. At 0730 the fire lifted and enemy infantry and tanks struck the left flank of Company E, along the railroad, and Company G, which was in contact with the 167 Brigade in the rough country west of the Albano road. Four tanks supporting the enemy infantry attacking Company G were knocked out by artillery fire and, with the exception of the 3d Platoon which was nearly wiped out, the company beat off every attempt to infiltrate its positions. Along the highway and railroad three enemy tanks and infantry broke through Company E's left platoon. One of the company's supporting tank destroyers was knocked out immediately; the other destroyed two of the enemy tanks and forced the third to retreat. Then it stopped the enemy infantry with its .50-caliber machine guns. All morning the company held. In the afternoon a squad of the right platoon was wiped out by tanks which destroyed the two supporting antitank guns and then moved directly into the platoon's positions. The enemy failed to press his advantage and the fighting died away toward evening.

Lighter blows fell upon the 180th Infantry, holding the right flank of the 45th Division front along the Carano road. A force of approximately two companies, following the numerous stream beds and ditches which drain to the south, attempted to infiltrate between Companies E and F. The regiment called for prearranged artillery defensive fires, and the artillery together with the machine guns of the forward companies mowed down the attacking troops. At nightfall, when the remnants of the two enemy companies were pulled back, they appeared to be completely disorganized. No deep penetrations had been made anywhere along the 45th Division front.

At the same time that the main enemy assault was directed against the 45th Division, diversionary attacks were launched against the 3d and 56 Divisions, holding the right and left flanks of the central beachhead defense line. In the 3d Division sector the enemy attacked at no less than six different points with forces ranging from single platoons to two companies. The principal attack came from the northwest of Ponte Rotto between the 2d Battalion, 7th Infantry, and the 3d Battalion, 30th Infantry. The first assault was launched by the *Parachute Demonstration Battalion,* attached to the *Hermann Goering Panzer Division,* supported by nine Mark IV tanks. The men in the two companies of the *Parachute Demonstration Battalion* were virtually all killed or captured; prisoners reported that men sick with dysentery had been forced into line for the attack. Accurate artillery fire drove back this first assault force in a state of disorder

bordering on panic. *Combat Group Berger,* in command of the attack, then committed its second wave, the *Hermann Goering Reconnaissance Battalion.* At one point the enemy penetrated 300 yards between Company K, 30th Infantry, and Company E, 7th Infantry. Company K was fighting from its command post when, at 1145, it called for an emergency barrage. The advance was stopped. The enemy kept up the pressure until midafternoon when heavy losses forced him to call a halt. The 751st Tank Battalion had knocked out five enemy tanks and a half-track; artillery and mortar fire accounted for scores of the infantry. By evening a counterattack had restored the 30th Infantry's original line.

Platoon- and company-strength attacks launched against the 509th Parachute Infantry Battalion on the 3d Division left flank were also repulsed without difficulty. On the division right flank the 504th Parachute Infantry was attacked by two companies which worked their way down Cisterna Creek from the north and another company which attacked from the southeast against the Mussolini Canal. The latter force was tied in with enemy units attacking the left flank of the 1st Special Service Force at the bridges near the junction of the west branch with the main Mussolini Canal. Although two outposts beyond the canal were wiped out, the enemy failed to cross the canal or to penetrate any part of the line, and again his losses were heavy. Company C, 894th Tank Destroyer Battalion, supporting the 1st Special Service Force, assisted the artillery in knocking out three tanks and a self-propelled gun. In front of Company D, 504th Parachute Infantry, losses were so heavy that in the afternoon the enemy requested an armistice to remove his casualties. An observer in Company D counted thirty-eight dead and estimated there were at least as many wounded.

On the 56 Division front the enemy's initial attacks had more success. The *3d Battalion, 12th (Sturm) Regiment,* attacked across the Moletta River against the 9 and 8 Royal Fusiliers. The enemy then shifted his emphasis farther to the east, striking from Buonriposo Ridge with ele-

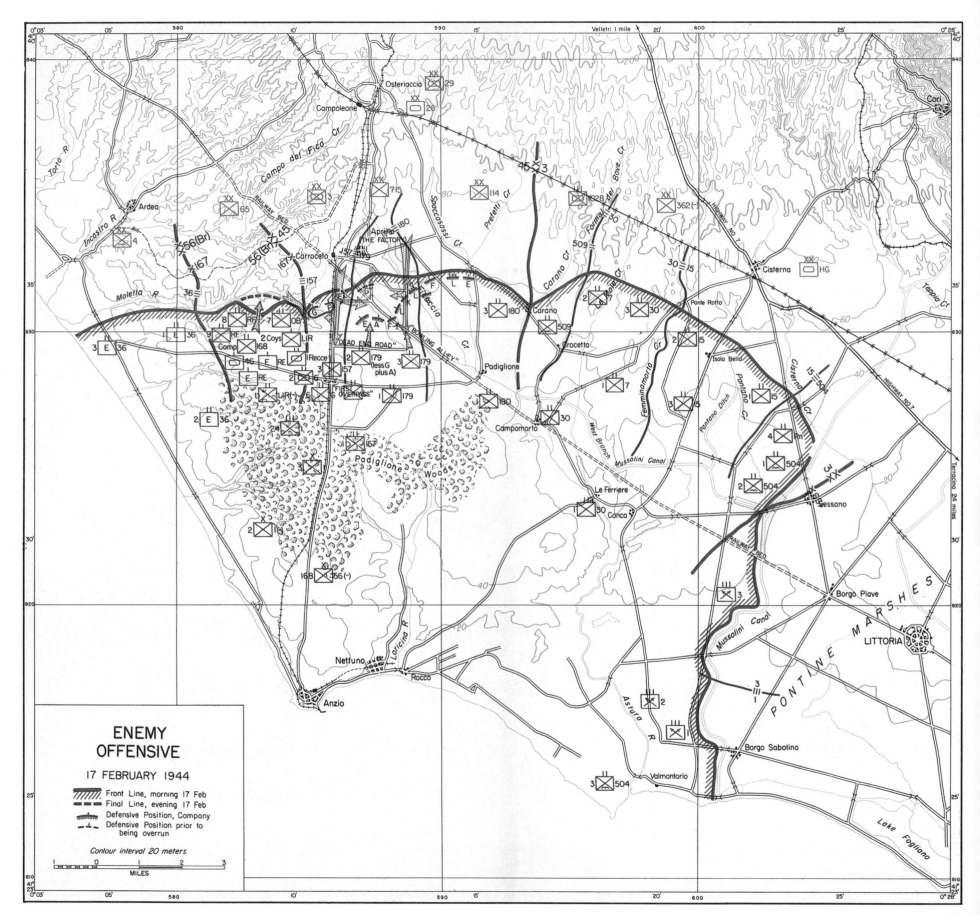

ENEMY
OFFENSIVE

17 FEBRUARY 1944

Front Line, morning 17 Feb
Final Line, evening 17 Feb
Defensive Position, Company
Defensive Position prior to
being overrun

Contour interval 20 meters

MILES

MAP NO. 16

ments of the *10th Parachute Regiment.* Two companies penetrated all the way to the lateral road along the final beachhead line before they were mopped up by tanks of the 46 Royal Tanks and the penetration checked by local counterattacks of the 8 Royal Fusiliers. The forward companies of the 8 Royal Fusiliers and the 7 Oxford Bucks were overrun, leaving the enemy holding a wedge in the center of the 167 Brigade line. No effort was made to exploit the penetration, and the 56 Division was given time to move up a composite battalion of the 168 Brigade for a counterattack. By noon it was apparent that the attack on the 56 Division was intended to do no more than support the major offensive down the Albano road.

In addition to laying down preparatory fire for the infantry attacks, enemy artillery on 16 February delivered the heaviest counterbattery fire yet experienced at the beachhead. In the early morning hours the fire was concentrated on the 45th Division artillery; then it shifted to the positions of the Corps artillery. At the same time a concerted effort was made to keep the highly respected cub observation planes on the ground. German pursuit planes added to their task of strafing Allied installations and forward troops the role of pursuing the vulnerable cubs. At 1000 the 3d Division reported that its observation plane had been shot down and that fighter protection was needed. VI Corps could guarantee no immediate aid. Enemy artillery had ranged in on the Nettuno air strip and destroyed four Spitfires as they were about to take off. The field had to be abandoned for use even during the daylight hours, and all fighter protection provided from fields in the Naples area.

Enemy planes and long-range guns concentrated on preventing supplies from entering the port. On 16 February the enemy air effort reached its peak with 19 missions and approximately 172 sorties. The results achieved were not commensurate with the effort expended. An ammunition dump north of Anzio was hit, but otherwise damage was slight. In contrast, XII Air Support Command reported 34 missions and 468 sorties flown in support of VI Corps. The main air effort, which had been planned

for the Cassino front, was shifted on short notice to the beachhead. From late morning to dark, wave after wave of fighter-bombers, light bombers, and medium bombers swept over the beachhead to attack assembly areas, troop concentrations, and tanks. The emphasis was placed on the 45th and 56 Division fronts, with dive bombers and medium bombers striking both the Factory and Carroceto, while heavy bombers worked over the communication lines feeding into the Rome area.

At the end of the first day of the big push the enemy had made only slight gains in the sectors of the 45th and 56 Divisions at considerable cost in tanks and personnel. It was evident that most of the attacks were intended only as diversions to wear down the strength of the defending troops and to pin reserves. The enemy had not yet committed his main force.

## The Second Day, 17 February

Before midnight on 16 February the enemy resumed the attack in the critical Albano road sector. (Map No. 16.) One company of the *725th Infantry Regiment (715th Infantry Division)* worked around both flanks of Company E, 157th Infantry, astride the road, while a second company infiltrated directly into Company E's positions. During the night the enemy slowly wiped out the forward positions from both the front and rear, forcing the remnants of the company into a small area around the command post. Here three tanks of the 191st Tank Battalion under the command of 1st Lt. Tommy L. Cobb, Jr., assisted them in holding out. The tanks fired their 75-mm. guns at point-blank range into the oncoming waves of troops and swept the surrounding fields with their .50-caliber machine guns. Before dawn Capt. Felix L. Sparks had only fourteen men left of his company and four men of Company H, his men were almost out of ammunition, and all supply routes were cut. Four enemy tanks were closing in on the flanks when at 0500 he received permission to withdraw to the west of the Albano road. With the aid of Lieutenant Cobb's M–4 Shermans, which knocked

BOMB CONCENTRATIONS ON CAMPOLEONE STATION *and
other targets along the railroad from Rome were in direct support of the
hard-pressed VI Corps troops. The smoke and dust of direct hits blanket
the station, while at the right a lone bomb hit straddles the tracks.*

out at least two of the enemy tanks, and a protective smoke screen laid down by the artillery, the handful of men fought its way out of the trap. The 2d Battalion, 179th Infantry, also under pressure during the night, sent a platoon west to contact the 157th Infantry, without success. A dangerous gap was opening up between the two regiments.

The enemy lost no time in exploiting the tactical advantage he had won by his successful night attack. Striking swiftly and in force he pressed through the gap he had opened along the Albano road. At 0740 an estimated thirty-five Focke-Wulf 190's and Messerschmitt 109's bombed and strafed the 45th Division's front line. A few minutes later both the 2d and 3d Battalions, 179th Infantry, were under attack by a powerful force composed of the *725th Infantry Regiment (715th Infantry Division)*, two battalions of the *145th Infantry Regiment (65th Infantry Division)*, and part of the *741st Infantry Regiment (114th Light Division)*. During the day approximately sixty tanks, employed in small groups, supported the infantry.

One force of tanks and infantry moved southeast from the Factory to attack the 3d Battalion along the north–south road a mile to the east of the Albano road, while a second force, after driving south from Carroceto along the highway, swung east through the former positions of Company E, 157th Infantry, to strike the 2d Battalion, 179th Infantry, in the flank. Company G, 179th Infantry, which had been under attack most of the night, was virtually isolated by this thrust. In order to protect his exposed left flank, the commander of the 179th Infantry, Colonel Kammerer, at 0855 ordered the 2d and 3d Battalions to withdraw 1,000 yards to the west branch of Carroceto Creek. Under cover of a smoke screen the 2d Battalion attempted to extricate itself from its untenable position. Company G was virtually destroyed; Companies E and F supported by Company A were unable to form a line until they had fallen back to the dead-end road less than a mile north of the final beachhead line. Again at 1040 thirty-five Focke-Wulf 190's and eight Messerschmitt 109's were over bombing and strafing. One bomb struck the 3d Battalion

command post, knocking out all communication lines. Tank destroyers and infantry fought desperately to hold off the enemy tanks, and the 4.2-inch mortars of the 83d Chemical Battalion grew hot as the sweating crews poured round after round into the seemingly unending waves of enemy infantry. At 0855, when the 3d Battalion had completed its move back to tie in with the 2d Battalion north of the dead-end road, the enemy had succeeded in driving a wedge two miles wide and over a mile deep into the center of the 45th Division front.

To aid the hard-pressed infantry, VI Corps brought to bear all the resources of its greatly superior artillery and air power. In addition to the 432 guns of Corps and division artillery, three companies of tanks from the 1st Armored Division and four batteries of 90-mm. antiaircraft guns were employed on ground targets, and two cruisers assisted with the fire of their naval guns on the flanks of the beachhead. All the resources of XII Air Support Command were put at the disposal of VI Corps. Counting only bombers, 198 fighter-bomber, 69 light-bomber, 176 medium-bomber, and 288 heavy-bomber sorties were flown in direct support of VI Corps. The heavy B–17 Flying Fortresses and B–24 Liberators and the Mitchell and Marauder medium bombers concentrated on Campoleone and targets up the Albano road; striking closer to the front lines, fighter-bombers blasted the already battered Factory, Carroceto, and the overpass; and during the hours of darkness armed reconnaissance planes and Wellington bombers patrolled all roads leading into the beachhead. The total weight of bombs dropped and the number of heavy bombers employed was the greatest up to that date ever allotted in direct support of an army. The term "direct support" was no misnomer for many of the big planes swinging in from the direction of Rome overshot their target at Campoleone and dropped their loads on the Factory, only a few hundred yards from the front lines. To the weary troops, looking up from the muddy blood-stained battlefield, the view of formation after formation of giant bombers sweeping majestically over the beachhead was a cheering sight.

During the afternoon the enemy attempted to broaden and deepen the salient he had won. Fresh troops were committed on the *3d Panzer Grenadier Division* front to bring the total enemy force involved to approximately fourteen infantry battalions. In most instances the attacks were made by small battle groups of battalion strength which were rotated frequently to keep fresh troops in the attack while units battered by the intense artillery fire and bombing were withdrawn to be reorganized. The main pressure continued to be exerted down the Albano road and to the east of it against the 2d and 3d Battalions, 179th Infantry. Tanks and infantry penetrated as far as the junction with the dead-end road where the tanks found conceal-

ment behind a group of farmhouses and the infantry proceeded to dig in. Two tanks broke through to the first overpass along the Albano road before they were stopped. On the west side of the highway the 2d Battalion, 157th Infantry, was almost surrounded by small groups of enemy infantry infiltrating through the deep ravines lying between the battalion and the 167 Brigade to the left. In the afternoon the regimental command post was bombed and communications broke down. When the lines were restored, the battalion reported that it was still intact. On the right shoulder of the salient, Company G, 180th Infantry, extended its left flank to maintain contact with Company K, 179th Infantry. Although it was in an exposed

THE FIRST OVERPASS ABOVE ANZIO, *where the east–west road crosses the main highway to Albano, was the scene of enemy artillery concentration as Allied tanks advanced northward to meet the counterattack on 17 February. A German tank (circled) can be seen at left center.*

position and under constant pressure, Company G held its ground. The enemy's efforts to widen the salient so far had failed.

Late in the morning of 17 February General Harmon was ordered to employ one battalion of medium tanks in a counterattack to support the 179th Infantry. Moving out shortly after noon Company H, 1st Armored Regiment, at 1410 reached the first overpass where the east–west road crosses the main highway. One platoon advanced 500 yards farther up the road and assisted in holding off the enemy tanks attacking toward the overpass. Company I followed the "bowling alley" across the open fields southeast of the Factory to support the 3d Battalion, 179th Infantry. Roadbound and under fire from enemy tank guns, it made little progress. At dusk both companies were withdrawn. They had assisted in holding off the enemy armor, but, unable to maneuver off the roads and lacking infantry support, the tanks were able to do little toward regaining the lost ground.

The enemy penetration down the Albano road had brought him dangerously near the final beachhead line of defense. In order to relieve some of the pressure on the 45th Division and to add depth to the defense, General Lucas assigned to the 1 Division, less the 3 Brigade which remained in Corps reserve, the task of holding a 2-mile sector of the final beachhead line of defense extending east and west from the first overpass on the Albano road. The 1 Division was tied in with the 56 Division on its left and the 1st Battalion, 179th Infantry, on its right. Corps also attached the 2d Battalion, 6th Armored Infantry, to the 45th Division. The battalion was placed under the control of the 157th Infantry and moved up to the first overpass, in position to relieve the 3d Battalion, 157th Infantry. The 56 Division strengthened its 167 Brigade with elements of the 168 Brigade which had been employed successfully that morning to wipe out the wedge the enemy had driven in the division's line the previous day. These shifts of units were accompanied by changes in personnel: Maj. Gen. G. W. R. Templer took command of both 56 and 1 Divisions when General Penney was wounded by a shell fragment, and General Truscott left the 3d Division to become Deputy Commander of VI Corps, his former position being filled by Brig. Gen. John W. O'Daniel.

In an effort to lessen the depth of the enemy penetration and to obtain a more defensible line, General Eagles ordered the 2d and 3d Battalions, 179th Infantry, and the 3d Battalion, 157th Infantry, to launch a counterattack on the night of 17–18 February. The 179th Infantry was to reach the west branch of the Carroceto Creek, an advance of 1,000 yards, while the 3d Battalion, 157th Infantry, was to reach a parallel position on the Albano road where it would be in position to tie in with the beleaguered 2d Battalion west of the highway. Maj. Asbury W. Lee's 191st Tank Battalion was to support the attack. At that time the 3d Battalion, 179th Infantry, had been reduced to 274 men and the 2d Battalion, even with Company A attached, was in little better condition. The two depleted battalions jumped off on schedule at 2300; the 3d Battalion, 157th Infantry, was delayed. Capt. Merle M. Mitchell, the battalion commander, had been wounded in the stomach and shoulder by enemy tank fire. Refusing to be evacuated he personally reconnoitered the route of advance and led his troops forward beyond the line of departure. Hampered by the necessity of using runners to maintain communications with his units and by pressure from the enemy, Captain Mitchell's attack did not get under way until 0030. The enemy had already succeeded in bringing up machine guns and consolidating his gains along the Albano road. The battalion encountered such heavy fire that it got no farther up the road than the junction with the dead-end road, almost 1,000 yards short of its objective. Lt. Col. Charles D. Wiegand, commanding the 2d Battalion, 179th Infantry, found his left flank exposed to attack from the west. Momentarily on the defensive, the enemy returned to the attack. Company E was partly cut off by enemy tanks and enemy infantry who came down the Albano road in half-tracks and unloaded at the corner of the dead-end road. Colonel Wiegand was forced to order a withdrawal. To the right, Companies K and L reached their objectives only to find that Company K was in a trap. The situation became confused. Enemy artillery fire knocked out all communications between the 2d Battalion and regimental headquarters making it difficult for Colonel Kammerer to keep abreast of the situation. The counterattack had failed. It lacked sufficient strength to throw the enemy off balance and it left the troops of the 179th Infantry in an exposed position.

## The Crisis, 18–19 February

All through the stormy night of 17–18 February the enemy moved up fresh units in preparation for a knockout blow, and even the counterattack launched by the 179th Infantry had not prevented him from continuing his customary tactics of infiltrating small groups under cover of darkness. During the night hours he paid special attention to the shoulders of the salient. On the left, enemy units, infiltrating along the ravines which drain into the Moletta River, got between the 167 Brigade and the 2d Battalion, 157th Infantry, cutting the battalion's supply route. On the right, Companies G and F of the 2d Battalion, 180th Infantry, holding the left flank along La Ficoccia Creek, were harassed by enemy tanks operating along the north–south road and enemy infantry infiltrating into their positions. Artillery fire worked over the units holding the final beachhead line. Behind this screen of activity the enemy completed preparations for what was to be his supreme effort to effect a breakthrough. During the day he was to employ all of the *721st, 741st,* and *735th Infantry Regiments,* and the *309th* and *29th Panzer Grenadier Regiments.* Armor continued to be used in small groups but on a more extensive scale than on any previous day. Each infantry unit had tank support; in the afternoon, when elements of the enemy reserve—the *26th Panzer* and *29th Panzer Grenadier Divisions*—were committed, tanks were employed with as many as twelve in a group. (Map No. 17.)

The enemy launched his first thrust at dawn. Capitalizing on the confusion resulting from the night infiltration and the unsuccessful Allied counterattack, he thrust deep into the positions of the 179th Infantry. Company K was virtually destroyed and only remnants of the 3d Battalion filtered back to the final beachhead line. Enemy tanks moved down the "bowling alley" until stopped by a blown bridge; enemy infantry infiltrating to the south and southeast reached the positions along the final beachhead line held by the 1 Loyals, east of the first overpass, and to its right by the 1st Battalion, 179th Infantry, and 1st Battalion, 180th Infantry. These initial attacks, which were not in great strength, were beaten off. For Company I of the 2d Battalion, 157th Infantry, which was holding a small area directly in front of the overpass, this was the second day of such attacks. The ring of barbed wire surrounding the company was littered with bodies of dead and moaning Germans who only a few moments before had been shouting confidently, "At ease, Company I," "Watch out, Company I, here we come!" Company I was also suffering terrific losses. Enemy 170-mm. and 210-mm. guns, registered on the overpass, blasted huge craters out of the swampy ground into which oozed muddy water to cover the torn remnants of what had been a rifleman or a machine-gun crew. One by one, five of Capt. James G. Evans' company officers were killed by the artillery fire and he was hard-pressed to find men to mend the breaks in the wire and man the machine guns covering the Albano road. Some ammunition reached the company during the night, but no food or water had been brought up for two days. The wounded had to be left in water-logged slit trenches where aid men gave them what help they could offer. Although the infantry attacks could be and were repulsed there was no relief from the cold, sleepless nights nor from the constant pounding the men were taking from artillery fire.

The 2d Battalion, 179th Infantry, almost cut off by the tank penetrations on its left and the collapse of the 3d Battalion on its right, withdrew under covering fire of Company A. By the middle of the morning the 179th Infantry had been driven back to the positions covering the final beachhead line.

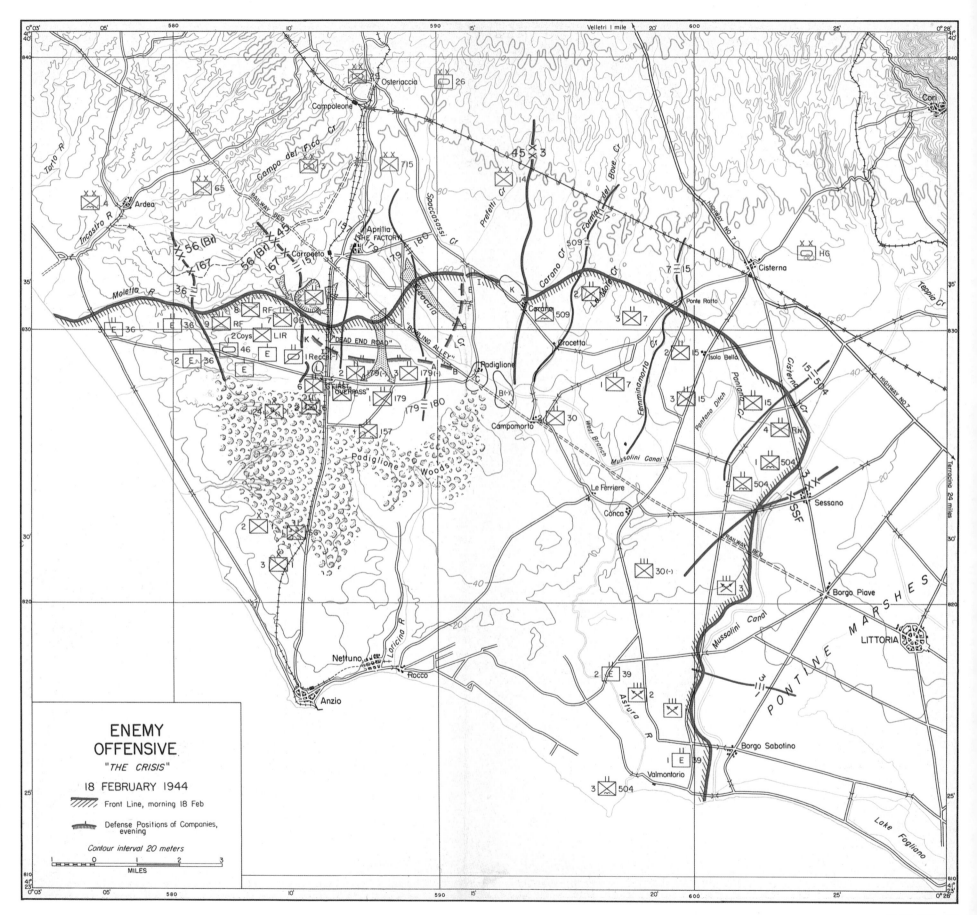

ENEMY
OFFENSIVE

"THE CRISIS"

18 FEBRUARY 1944

Front Line, morning 18 Feb

Defense Positions of Companies,
evening

Contour interval 20 meters

MILES

MAP NO. 17

To its right the 2d Battalion, 180th Infantry, was under attack from three sides by enemy tanks operating along the roads east of the Factory. Companies F and G at 0625 were ordered to withdraw a half mile to the east. Company F, led by Capt. Robert A. Guenthner, and a platoon of Company G extricated themselves; 1st Lt. Benjamin A. Blackmer who had taken over command of Company G never received the order. Completely surrounded, the company fought off every enemy effort to overrun it. On the other shoulder of the salient the beleaguered 2d Battalion, 157th Infantry, virtually cut off from all support, likewise held. Although the enemy had widened his penetration and driven it a half mile deeper into the positions of the 45th Division, the courage and staying power of the American infantrymen still stood in the way of a breakthrough.

The bloody struggle continued all morning under an overcast sky which prevented a repetition of the previous day's tremendous program of air support. Fighter-bombers, which flew 120 sorties, gave effective close support against enemy tanks and infantry, and twenty-four light bombers covered the Factory area with fragmentation bombs. Medium and heavy bombers were unable to get off the ground. However, there was no reduction in the amount of artillery fire which fell on the attacking troops. Many of the Allied artillery ground observers became casualties or had their radios and telephones shot out, but the enemy's efforts to keep down the cub observation planes failed. At 1110 Capt. William H. McKay, a cub pilot observing for the 45th Division artillery, spotted a force of tanks and about 2,500 Germans moving south from Carroceto along the Albano road, and radioed the news to the artillery. Within twelve minutes the Corps Fire Control Center had massed the fire of 224 British and American guns on the target. The ground over which the Germans were marching seemed to blow up and when the smoke cleared the enemy force had disintegrated. In the next fifty minutes, under the direction of Captain McKay, the concentrated fire of these guns was shifted to four other locations. Many enemy units were disorgan-

ized and decimated before they were even in position to attack, yet there appeared to be no end to the waves of enemy infantry thrown against the 45th Division.

At 1400, when Col. William O. Darby took command of the 179th Infantry, the situation appeared desperate. The shattered 3d Battalion had been withdrawn for reorganization, the 2d Battalion was at less than half strength and nearly exhausted. Only the 1st Battalion was capable of organized resistance. All communication lines between the regiment and its battalions were out, further complicating the task of creating a coordinated defense. Calling together his battalion commanders Colonel Darby ordered Colonel Johnson to hold the left sector with his 1st Battalion, reinforced with Company I; Colonel Wiegand, commander of the 2d Battalion, was to take over the right sector "with whatever troops he could find," and Maj. Merlin O. Tyron, commander of the 3d Battalion, was to "endeavor to get all stragglers and pick all men physically fit in the rear echelon." Colonel Darby favored falling back to the woods to reorganize. General Eagles replied to the request with an order to hold the final beachhead line at all costs and he promised the support of the 1st Battalion, 157th Infantry.

The 180th Infantry, on the right flank, was still largely intact, but its units were holding a long front exposed to enemy tank attacks and Company G was completely cut off. The enemy's tanks could operate almost at will down the Albano road and the "bowling alley." A large percentage of the division's antitank guns had been knocked out or overrun during the fighting of the past three days; the tanks of the 191st Tank Battalion and the tank destroyers of the 645th Tank Destroyer Battalion had suffered heavy losses while beating off the seemingly endless succession of enemy attacks. The 645th Tank Destroyer Battalion alone lost fourteen M–10's on 17 February. In order to obtain full defilade it was often necesssary to dig the tank destroyers into the marshy ground. Once in place they were difficult to move and in some cases they had to be abandoned when the infantry withdrew.

In the late afternoon of 18 February, as the enemy prepared to make his heaviest attack of the day, the Allied defenders of the Anzio beachhead faced their most critical test.

The renewed enemy attack started with a thrust by twelve tanks down the "bowling alley." Only the blown bridge where the road crosses Carroceto Creek kept them from breaking through. Strung out along the road the tanks were able to fire directly into the fox holes of Company A, 180th Infantry. Under the cover of this fire the enemy infantry attacked. By 1750 the fighting was general along the whole front of the salient as far west as the overpass. Both Company A, 180th Infantry, and the 1st and 2d Battalions, 179th Infantry, held their ground. Small enemy units managed to infiltrate through the area of heavy brush growing along the regimental boundary north of the road where the line of defending troops was thin. The enemy force had been whittled down until it was too weak to exploit its penetration and the infiltrating units were wiped out during the night. Farther to the west the 1st Battalion, 179th Infantry, and the 1 Loyals were attacked by enemy troops who came in across the open fields south of the dead-end road. For four hours the enemy troops fought to break through east of the overpass. At one time they penetrated all the way to the lateral road before they were driven back in hand-to-hand fighting. Tanks of the 1st Armored Division, patrolling the lateral road, helped the infantry hold off the enemy until the force of the attacks was spent. Compelled to advance across open country, the enemy was taking terrific casualties from artillery, mortar, and machine-gun fire. At 2130 there was evidence that the enemy was pulling back to reorganize. Never again was he to come so close to rolling up the final beachhead line.

During the night of 18–19 February, the 45th Division took advantage of a temporary lull in the enemy attacks to strengthen its positions while VI Corps assembled a counterattack force. (Map No. 18.) West of the Albano road the 2d Battalion, 6th Armored Infantry, under the command of Lt. Col. Wilhelm P. Johnson, managed to break through

to the 2d Battalion, 157th Infantry, making it possible to send supplies and ammunition forward to the beleaguered troops. General Eagles released the 1st Battalion, 157th Infantry, from division reserve and attached it to the 179th Infantry. The fresh troops were employed to relieve the decimated 2d Battalion, 179th Infantry, along the lateral road, thereby strengthening the final beachhead line at a critical point. Behind the line Major Tyron reorganized the remnants of the 3d Battalion, 179th Infantry, and reinforced them with 250 men who were brought up from rear areas. Combat groups organized within the 2d and 3d Battalions were prepared for use in bolstering the 1st Battalion. On the left of the 179th Infantry the 1 Loyals adopted the same policy of pressing rear-echelon troops into service to replace casualties. To give more armored support Company F, 1st Armored Regiment, moved into position along the lateral road where it could support the infantry.

The 180th Infantry, holding the right shoulder of the salient, also took advantage of the night hours to readjust its line. The forward companies were drawn back from the north and west to a shorter line extending from just north of the lateral road to the village of Carano. Although the regiment had been under constant artillery fire and local tank and infantry attacks, its losses had been comparatively light. Even the troops of Company G fought their way out of the trap where they had been held throughout the daylight hours of 18 February. Lieutenant Blackmer's company had been reduced by the withdrawal of the 3d Platoon and by casualties until there were barely fifty men left. Communication lines to the rear had been cut, the radio was damaged, and there were no supplies; there were no grenades, no mortar shells, and only a few rounds left for the rifles and machine guns. Four of the company officers had been evacuated on the first night of the attack and many of the men were beginning to suffer from trench foot. Exposed in no man's land, the tiny force was subject to friendly artillery fire as well as to enemy attacks. At 1430 Lieutenant Blackmer ordered his men to pull back 300 yards farther down La Ficoc-

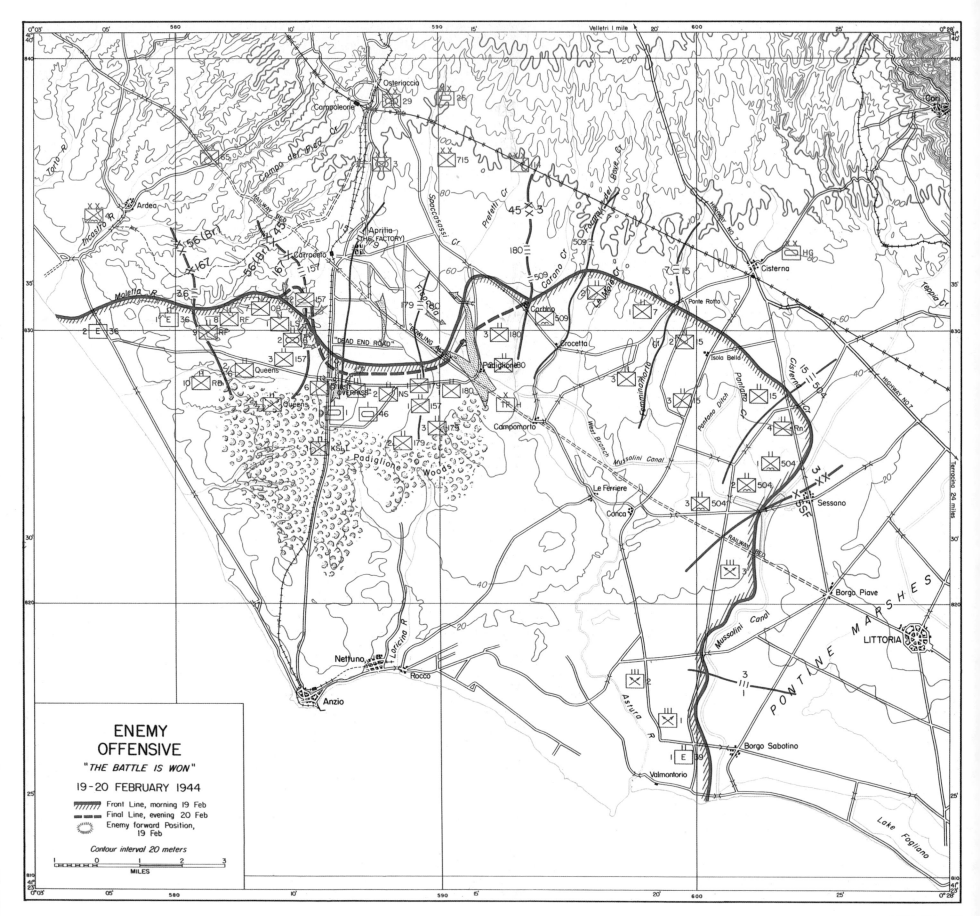

ENEMY
OFFENSIVE

"THE BATTLE IS WON"

19-20 FEBRUARY 1944

Front Line, morning 19 Feb
Final Line, evening 20 Feb
Enemy forward Position,
19 Feb

Contour interval 20 meters

1  0  1  2  3
MILES

MAP NO. 18

cia Creek; but Allied artillery spotted his position and began firing on the company. Pfc. William J. Johnston, a machine gunner, was left for dead by his comrades. Though seriously wounded Johnston attempted to crawl back up the stream bank to his gun. A passing soldier assisted him and he resumed firing in an effort to hold off the enemy while his company organized its new position. At 1600 Pfc. Robert Keefe, a company runner, reached battalion headquarters and then crawled back through the enemy lines with orders for Lieutenant Blackmer to withdraw. After dark the company fought its way through the enemy units dug in to its rear and waded over a mile through the waist-deep water of the creek to reach the regiment's new line

of defense. By some miracle Johnston also managed to crawl back to safety the next morning. The spirit of these men could not be broken. When Colonel Dulaney called 2d Battalion headquarters to find out about Company G, he was told that "Blackmer came out grinning." The atmosphere of confusion and desperation which had marked the fighting during the late afternoon hours of 18 February was changing to a spirit of confidence as the 45th Division reestablished an integrated line of defense, and communication between units was restored.

In view of the possibility that the enemy might employ airborne troops in conjunction with a continuation of his infantry and tank attacks, VI

TANKS MOVE UP THE ALBANO Road *on 19 February from Padiglione Woods toward the front lines where smoke obscures the lateral road. These units of the 1st Armored Division were going forward in support of the 45th Division's stand to halt the German drive in that sector.*

ENGINEERS BRIDGE A STREAM *on a road from Nettuno to the front. Frequent rains and enemy shell-fire damage made this a difficult task, but the roads had to be kept open to move armor against the Germans.*

Corps, on the afternoon of 18 February, issued an order dividing the beachhead area into zones of defense against airborne attacks. Forward zones were made the responsibility of the units holding the beachhead line of defense; responsibility for the rear areas was divided among the 35th Anti-aircraft Artillery Brigade, the 18th Field Artillery Brigade, the 39th Engineers, and the 1st Special Service Force. Within each zone a mobile force of at least one company was to be held on the alert, and all roads were to be patrolled constantly during the hours of darkness. By employing reconnaissance units and rear-echelon troops for the anti-parachutist patrols, the drain on the critically short supply of infantry units was kept to a minimum.

The enemy devoted the night hours of 18–19 February to assembling his forces for what was to be his last serious effort to break through the final beachhead line of defense. (Map No. 18.) At 0400 on the morning of 19 February enemy medium- and heavy-caliber artillery fire was laid down along the forward edge of the salient, followed ten minutes later by an infantry attack. The 45th Division artillery replied with prepared defensive

fires, concentrating on the front of the 1st Battalion, 179th Infantry, and the 1 Loyals. Two battalions of the enemy's reserve *15th Panzer Grenadier Regiment (29th Panzer Grenadier Division),* supported by three tanks, overran the right flank company of the 1 Loyals and penetrated to the lateral road. The remainder of the 1 Loyals and the 179th Infantry stood firm. By 0800, pounded by shells from the tank guns of Company F, 1st Armored Regiment, and by a tremendous concentration of artillery fire, the enemy was forced to withdraw, leaving only a pocket of resistance around a group of houses on the lateral road. During the morning, enemy tanks tried repeatedly and unsuccessfully to operate down the Albano road. Destroyers of the 701st Tank Destroyer Battalion knocked out two Mark VI Tigers and five Mark IV's. At noon when the enemy tried a final infantry attack down the same axis it was effectively broken up by artillery fire before any contact had been made. Although there was an increase in the enemy air effort over the previous day, marked by repeated bombing and strafing raids over the forward lines, the peak of the enemy offensive had been passed.

### The Battle is Won, 19–20 February

While the enemy was regrouping for his last effort to crack the final beachhead line of defense, VI Corps completed preparations for a counterattack. The plan called for an attack to drive the enemy back to a line extending in an arc from the stream crossing just north of the junction of the dead-end and Albano roads eastward and slightly northward toward the village of Carano. Two forces were to be employed: Force T, under General Templer, consisting of the 169 Brigade, was to attack on Corps order from the vicinity of the overpass to seize the ground north of the dead-end road; Force H, under General Harmon, consisting of the 6th Armored Infantry (less the 2d

PRISONERS FORMED LONG COLUMNS *as they were marched single file from the battle area. Passing a group of curious American infantrymen on 19 February, these German captives, including men from the 114 Light Division, displayed little interest in their captors.*

Battalion), a battalion of medium tanks, and the 30th Infantry, which was moved over from the less active 3d Division front, was to attack at 0630 on 19 February up the "bowling alley" to the junction with the first north–south road. The original intention was to have the two forces attack simultaneously to pinch off the enemy troops in the nose of the salient. Inability on the part of Force T to assemble its equipment before the time scheduled necessitated a modification of the plan to a limited objective attack by Task Force H. (Map No. 18.) On the night of 17-18 February enemy planes dropped naval mines in the harbor of Anzio. The port was closed until the mines were cleared and the newly arrived 169 Brigade was delayed in unloading its equipment. Thus on February 19 only Task Force H was prepared to jump off when dawn broke on what promised to be a clear, warm day.

The artillery carried out an elaborate fire plan to support the attack. Eight British field artillery regiments were coordinated to fire a supporting barrage which was laid down in front of the line of departure at 0600 and then lifted on call. In addition, eight battalions of Corps artillery fired prepared concentrations for forty-five minutes on enemy assembly areas north and east of the Factory. Naval and 90-mm. antiaircraft guns fired on the Factory and Carroceto, while fighter-bombers and medium bombers, part of a large air support program, likewise blasted assembly areas. One wooded area northeast of the Factory was struck by 132 fighter-bombers and 48 medium bombers, and another 48 mediums scattered fragmentation bombs on an assembly area along the stream to the north of the woods.

Force H attacked on schedule at 0630. Colonel Steele's 6th Armored Infantry and Colonel McGarr's 30th Infantry advanced abreast along the axis of the "bowling alley" with the 6th Armored Infantry south of the road and the 30th Infantry, in column of battalions, astride and north of the road.

Col. Louis V. Hightower, commander of the 1st Armored Regiment, employed two medium tank companies: Company G in direct support of the infantry and Company H assisting on the right flank. The attack started well. At 0820 the 30th Infantry had advanced a mile beyond the line of departure, and the armored infantry on its left was meeting only slight resistance. Then the advance slowed. The 2d Battalion, leading the 30th Infantry, was under fire from enemy Mark VI tanks as well as from troops concealed along the banks of La Ficoccia Creek and in the brush on the north side of the road. Lt. Col. Lyle W. Bernard was wounded and Lt. Col. Woodrow W. Stromberg took over the 2d Battalion. Company E was reduced to one officer and fifty men and Company F also was badly chewed up. The tanks of Company G, 1st Armored Regiment, could offer little assistance as they were held up until the engineers completed work on a bridge. At 1330 the attack was resumed. Company G's tanks crossed the repaired bridge and drove up the diagonal road spreading panic among the already disorganized enemy troops. The tanks of Company H also were successful. After advancing over a mile up the road leading north from Padiglione, they turned west to cover the bridge across Spaccasassi Creek. Blasting the enemy infantry from the stream bed and from houses along the road, they took so many prisoners that they had to call on the 180th Infantry to dispose of them. At 1620, 19 February, when General Harmon called a halt to the advance, the infantry had reached the objective called for in VI Corps' order. The main assault force was withdrawn during the night. Two battalions, left as a covering force, engaged in aggressive patrolling throughout 20 February and then were withdrawn. In its attack, Force H captured two hundred prisoners representing elements of the *741st, 721st,* and *735th Infantry Regiments* and a company of the *114th Engineer Battalion.*

During the afternoon of 19 February the 1 Loyals and a company of the 2 North Staffs, supported by tanks of the 46 Royal Tank Regiment, attacked to wipe out the pocket of resistance along the lateral road left by the enemy's penetration in the morning. At 1600 the houses in which the enemy troops had barricaded themselves were re-taken. An hour earlier a platoon of Company D, 1st Armored Regiment, drove up the Albano road almost to the junction with the dead-end road. Its mission was to cause as much confusion and damage as possible. Three of the tanks were knocked out by enemy antitank guns, and the remaining tanks were forced to withdraw under cover of a smoke screen. Before pulling back, the platoon assisted the British counterattack by driving a large force of the enemy from cover. The British took over 200 prisoners, who together with the prisoners taken by Force H, brought the total for the day to 413. General Lucas signalized the victory with a message to his troops: "Swell work today. Keep after them."

The decline in the size of the forces, both in infantry and in tanks, which the enemy employed in his attacks on the morning of 19 February, the large number and the variety of units represented by the prisoners taken during the counterattacks, and above all the picture of disorganization within units and the spirit of disillusionment exhibited by the enemy prisoners indicated that VI Corps by the evening of 19 February had won its battle. It was anticipated that the enemy would keep up the pressure, for the prestige of the German Army was at stake. It was considered possible that General Mackensen would attempt another major effort to break through to the sea. Still, all the evidence on 19 February pointed to the conclusion that the German *Fourteenth Army* was too near the point of exhaustion to continue the battle on the scale of the past three days without either bringing up additional fresh troops or pausing for a period of rest and reorganization. Since the enemy had already committed elements of the *26th Panzer* and *29th Panzer Grenadier Divisions,* which he had intended to hold in reserve to exploit a breakthrough, it was believed unlikely that he had many fresh troops left.

The fighting on 20 February only served to buttress the conclusion that VI Corps had broken the back of the enemy offensive. At 0430 an enemy force estimated at company strength attacked the

1 Loyals east of the overpass. The attack was easily repulsed. Prisoners taken from the *67th Panzer Grenadier Regiment (26th Panzer Division)* reported that the attack had started with a battalion but that artillery fire had broken it up and only a company had reached the Allied lines. Prisoners taken later in the morning by the 179th Infantry revealed a condition of even greater confusion in the ranks of the *29th Panzer Grenadier Division.* According to the prisoners from the *71st Panzer Grenadier Regiment,* both the *71st* and *45th Panzer Grenadier Regiments* were to have attacked at 0400, 19 February. Disrupted communications had caused such confusion in the transmission of orders that the *71st Panzer Grenadier Regiment* failed to attack until the morning of 20 February. Leaving its assembly area north of the Factory in the early morning hours, the *1st Battalion* of the regiment had advanced into the no man's land in the center of the salient. Under fire from all directions, the companies became confused, lost their bearings, and became hopelessly mixed up. The battalion commander called a halt to reconnoiter. He found that the *15th Panzer Grenadier Regiment,* which was supposed to be on his right, was to his rear; the two connecting companies had been destroyed; and the *3d Battalion* of his own regiment had failed to follow up. Left isolated and under terrific artillery fire, the battalion disintegrated. Although the enemy continued his attacks on the shoulders of the salient, the debacle on the morning of 20 February marked a bloody end to his efforts to achieve a breakthrough.

The German forces lost heavily both in personnel and equipment during their drive to wipe out the Anzio beachhead. In their 5-day attack, 16–20 February, the enemy suffered at least 5,389 battle casualties in killed, wounded, and missing. Enemy prisoners taken by VI Corps numbered 609. The German High Command never hesitated to sacrifice troops to achieve an important objective, and the elimination of the beachhead had become as much a question of prestige as of military strategy. On 21 February the 179th Infantry counted about 500 bodies lying in front of its sector. An escaped

THE GERMAN "GOLIATH" TANK, *the enemy's secret weapon which proved a failure, was nothing more than a miniature mobile explosives container. On the side of this "Goliath" can be seen the battery from which power was drawn to operate the motor at the right.*

American prisoner reported that while being marched up the Albano road he had seen enemy dead stacked up like cordwood in piles of 150 each. Bulldozers were being employed to dig mass graves for what he estimated to be over 1,500 bodies. Most of the German units which entered the bitterly contested corridor along the Albano road had to be withdrawn for a period of rest and rehabilitation.

The successful battle fought by the Allied troops to hold their beachhead was won at a price lower than that paid by the enemy, but still high enough to cause concern to the already depleted units of VI Corps. Although the landing of new units in the period 16–20 February increased the effective strength of VI Corps from 86,915 to 96,401, the beachhead forces still numbered 21,268 less than their authorized strength. During this period, battle casualties totaled 3,496 in killed, wounded, and missing. The Germans reported the capture of 1,304 Allied prisoners. Exposure, exhaustion, and particularly trench foot resulting from days spent in fox holes half-filled with water resulted in a total of 1,637 nonbattle casualties. Although high, the losses suffered by VI Corps would not have been serious had it been possible to draw the troops out of the line for a period of recuperation. During February there were no quiet periods at the beachhead. Every man was needed and the steady drain on the lives and energy of the defending troops never ceased.

The enemy had started his all-out drive to destroy the beachhead with many advantages. VI Corps was forced to defend a front of nearly thirty-five miles with less than five divisions of troops, many of whom had been in the line continuously for nearly a month; at the same time it had to maintain an adequate reserve. General Mackensen, with nearly ten divisions under his command, had the larger force, and many of his troops were fresher. Nor were the enemy's artillery and air power negligible factors. By concentrating his artillery fire on the area around the salient on either side of the Albano road he was able to subject the troops under attack to a merciless pounding, and the congested area of the beachhead offered an excellent target for his bombers. In spite of these advantages he had failed, because of the Allied superiority in artillery and air power, the inability of the enemy to employ his tanks in masses, the failure of his secret weapon (the "Goliath" remote-controlled tank), the breakdown of enemy morale, and, finally, the stubborn resistance of the Allied troops holding the beachhead.

Prisoners taken during the battle almost invariably commented on the "terrific" and "continuous" artillery fire, which caused heavy casualties, shattered nerves, destroyed morale, and brought some units to the verge of panic. In a report to Field Marshal Kesselring of 28 February, General Mackensen stated that artillery fire was responsible for the bulk of enemy casualties, and that 75 percent of all wounds had been inflicted by shell frag-

ments. In many cases attacking troops were completely cut off from any support; communication between units was dependent almost entirely on radio and on runners, many of whom never lived to deliver their messages. In some cases, as a result of the breakdown of supply services, units went for days without food. At the peak of the attack, for every shell the enemy artillery fired, VI Corps threw back from fifteen to twenty. The salient the enemy had driven into the 45th Division front became a veritable death trap for his tanks and infantry.

The Allied air bombing and artillery fire served to complement each other. An appreciable share of the responsibility for the breakdown of communications and the failure of supplies to reach forward units was due to the weight of bombs dropped along the axis of the Albano road from the Factory and Carroceto back to the Albano hills. Straining his reserves to the utmost, the enemy was able to fly an estimated total of 172 sorties on 16 February, the peak day of his performance. The next day 288 Allied heavy bombers alone were over the beachhead. Whereas the number of enemy sorties steadily declined the Allied air effort was curtailed only by bad weather and lack of targets.

Many enemy prisoners attributed their failure to lack of adequate tank support. This was due partly to losses suffered during the fighting, but largely to unfavorable tank terrain. Both enemy and Allied tanks were roadbound and consequently could be employed only in small groups. In some cases the lead tank and rear tank of a column were knocked out, blocking the escape of the remainder; wherever tanks were used in groups of more than two or three they made excellent targets for artillery. At no time did tanks prove a crucial factor in the final result of the battle, although the prisoners paid tribute to the effectiveness with which the 1st Armored Division tanks were employed in the counterattacks on 19 February.

The enemy's touted secret weapon, the Goliath tank, proved to be a dud. This was a squat miniature tank loaded with explosive and designed to breach obstacles such as mine fields, barbed wire, and concrete walls. The tanks were controlled and exploded by electrical impulses transmitted through a long cable. But for the capture of prisoners, VI Corps troops during the period of the offensive would not have been aware of the midget tank's presence at the beachhead. According to an engineer of the *813th Engineer Company*, which was sent to the beachhead expressly for the offensive, the Goliaths were employed only on the first day of the attack, when thirteen of them bogged down; of these, three were blown up by Allied artillery fire and the other ten were dragged away.

The morale of the enemy troops declined rapidly as the attack bogged down. They had been promised an easy victory. The *29th Panzer Grenadier Division* went into the battle in high spirits. The troops had heard rumors that large numbers of Allied prisoners had been taken, that the attack was progressing favorably, that for once the German Air Force would not be busy on another front, and that they would be able to fight with tanks again. When they were subjected to Allied bombing and arrived on the front in the midst of what a prisoner called "carnage," they lost all desire to continue the attack. They felt they had been deceived and their morale suffered accordingly.

The fighting spirit of the individual Allied soldier played an important part in the successful defense of the beachhead. During the dark hours of 18 February when the enemy infantry seemed to be infiltrating everywhere, when communications broke down, and when whole companies and battalions were cut off, it was the will to win of the Allied troops which gave them the strength to hold. With this spirit, the men of VI Corps had won the major battle in defense of the beachhead.

# VI CORPS HOLDS THE BEACHHEAD
## (20 February–3 March)

Although the major enemy offensive to drive VI Corps into the sea had been repulsed, the Germans had no intention of abandoning their ultimate objective of annihilating the Anzio beachhead. Convinced that an immediate continuation of the frontal attack down the Albano road would be futile, the enemy turned his attention to the shoulders of the salient he had driven into the center of the beachhead defenses. At first, the Germans planned to mass their available forces against the eastern flank of the salient, along Spaccassasi Creek above Padiglione; but on 20 February they decided to concentrate on the western shoulder below Buonriposo Ridge. The Germans hoped that, by wearing down the shoulders of the salient, they would weaken the Allied forces holding the central beachhead defense sector so that the frontal attack down the Albano road could be successfully renewed.

Many German units suffered such heavy losses in the assaults of 16-20 February that they had lost their offensive punch. By 19 February, the combat strength of the *65th Infantry Division* was only 901 officers and men, and 4 days later this figure had been reduced to 673. The *735th Infantry Regiment* of the *715th Infantry Division* had only 185 officers and men on 20 February; this remnant was assigned to the *725th Infantry Regiment,* which was itself severely depleted and had to be withdrawn from the front on 23 February. Under such circumstances, the Germans had to pause to regroup and replenish their forces before they could again launch a large-scale attack.

In view of the apparent German intention to continue the offensive, General Clark sent a message to General Lucas on 20 February urging him to make every effort to strengthen the weakened beachhead defenses. General Clark was particularly concerned about the shoulders of the salient, where the 157th and 180th Infantry's stubborn refusal to give ground had been a major factor in containing the enemy's drive. Steps were taken to reduce the front held by the exhausted regiments of the 45th Division and to organize effective reserve positions.

In the two days after the successful counterattack launched by Force H on the morning of 19 February, the 6th Armored Infantry (less the 2d Battalion) and the 30th Infantry were withdrawn to positions near Padiglione and Campomorto and placed in Corps reserve. Here they were in position to support the 180th Infantry on the right shoulder of the salient. On 22 February one battalion of the 30th Infantry reverted to the 3d Division, the boundary between the 45th and 3d Divisions was moved 1,500 yards west from Carano, and the 3d Battalion, 30th Infantry, took over this new sector, thereby shortening the front of the 180th Infantry and adding strength to the critical shoulder.

Responsibility for the left shoulder of the salient passed to the 1 and 56 Divisions. The 1 Division relieved the 3d Battalion, 157th Infantry, and the 2d Battalion, 6th Armored Infantry, in position north of the overpass and west of the Albano road. The 56 Division was given responsibility for relieving the 2d Battalion, 157th Infantry, which had succeeded in beating off every enemy attempt to destroy its hold on the anchor position of the left shoulder.

The effect of the shift of boundaries was to reduce the front of the 45th Division by nearly one-half. The division took steps immediately to reorganize its units and strengthen the final beachhead line by assisting in the construction of a new Corps reserve line, 2,000 yards south of the lateral road. A series of battalion positions was laid out and the work of preparing them for defense divided among the units in reserve. On 19 February VI Corps ordered the 35th Antiaircraft Artillery Brigade to assemble a force of 30 officers and 650 enlisted men to work on defenses and to be on 2-hour alert for use as Corps reserve. Under the direction of the 120th Engineer Combat Battalion the antiaircraft troops assisted the 45th Division in constructing new reserve positions in the wooded areas a mile to the south of the final beachhead line. At the same time, by rotating the units in the line, the 45th Division was able to rehabilitate its depleted and tired troops, absorb new replacements, and rebuild its efficiency as a fighting unit.

The 1 and 56 Divisions, which were now responsible for the left shoulder of the salient, also adopted a policy of rotating the forward troops in line. Lack of adequate replacements made it difficult to build up units depleted during the fighting for Campoleone and the Factory area as well as by the big attack. The brigades of the 1 Division were far below strength, and the 56 Division had only one brigade, the 169, which was fresh. Heavy fighting during the period 20–25 February further reduced the effective strength of the two divisions, and only the arrival of the 18 Brigade on 25 February, which was attached to the 1 Division, prevented the situation from becoming critical. With the aid of the additional troops, work was rushed on new defenses to tie in with the 45th Division, while every effort was made to improve the old positions in the forward areas. The latter task was complicated by almost continuous pressure from the enemy against the shoulders of the salient.

## The Battle of the Caves

The left shoulder of the salient was held throughout the period of the big offensive by the 157th Infantry (less the 1st Battalion), assisted by the 2d Battalion, 6th Armored Infantry. (Map No. 18.) The troops were under almost constant fire for six days and it was imperative that they be relieved if the hold on the left shoulder was to be maintained. On the night of 21–22 February, 1 Division troops moved up to effect the relief of the 3d Battalion, 157th Infantry, and the 2d Battalion, 6th Armored Infantry, in position north of the first overpass and west of the Albano road. Not much remained of Company I, 157th Infantry. Of the 8 officers and 159 enlisted men with which he had entered the battle Captain Evans could find only 3 officers and 68 men to lead out of his small area of shell-cratered ground north of the overpass. The rest of his men had either been captured, blown to bits by artillery fire, or had died fighting to prevent the enemy infantry from crawling through the barbed wire protecting the company area. The 1 Division occupied its new positions without any immediate reaction from the enemy; the 56 Division which was assigned the task of relieving the 2d Battalion, 157th Infantry, was less fortunate. It became involved in what came to be known as the battle of the caves.

At the beginning of the German offensive on 16 February, the 2d Battalion, 157th Infantry, under the command of Lt. Col. Laurence C. Brown, was covering a front of over 2,000 yards extending from a point 500 yards east of the Albano road into a maze of deep ravines from which flow the headwaters of the Moletta River west of the highway. (Maps No. 15 and 16.) Enemy tanks, driving down the Albano road, rolled up the battalion right flank; enemy infantry, infiltrating up the

THE CAVES, *scene of bitter fighting on the left of the beachhead,*
*are graphically depicted in this sketch by soldier-artist Mitchell Siporin.*

ravines, overran the left flank and repeatedly cut the battalion's supply route to the south. As squads and platoons were cut off one by one, the battalion was finally reduced to a small area 600 yards west of the highway where a series of caves provided a natural fortress. On the night of 18–19 February the enemy got close enough to throw hand grenades into the battalion command post. Friendly artillery fire was called down on the caves and the draws around them, effectively breaking up the attack. That night, following the successful attack by the 2d Battalion, 6th Armored Infantry, supplies were brought up. The next night one hundred wounded were evacuated. From then on the battalion was virtually cut off. By preventing the enemy from widening the salient the battalion had aided materially in saving the beachhead, but fresh troops were needed if the position was to be held.

It was important that VI Corps retain control of the left shoulder and particularly of the network of dirt roads leading south to the final beachhead line. Once the enemy broke through to the lateral road west of the overpass he would be in position to cut the main supply route for the troops holding the Moletta River line.

Unfortunately the attempt of General Templer to relieve the trapped battalion coincided with the enemy's decision to continue the offensive in an area where rough terrain favored infiltration. On the night of 21 February the 2/7 Queens[1] (56 Division) reached the caves. On the way up the column was bombed and shelled and the supply train was held up by enemy opposition. An effort

---

[1] The second battalion organized in the British Army which bore the designation: "7 Battalion, The Queen's Royal Regiment (West Surrey)."

to send tanks and antitank guns up the main highway also failed with the loss of three tanks and
one gun. The British troops reached the caves without supplies, ammunition, or supporting weapons
and they had suffered about seventy casualties.
When they took over the positions guarding the
approaches to the caves, they had to be equipped
with American automatic weapons. Then the
enemy attacked. Capt. George O. Hubbert, artillery
liaison officer with the battalion, called for the
artillery concentration which had been fired on
the night of 18–19 February and again the draws
around the caves were filled with exploding shells
and the moans of wounded Germans. The enemy
assault was broken up, but it was impossible for
the 2d Battalion to leave the caves that night.

Fighting continued all day on 22 February while
the British completed the task of occupying their
new positions and the 2d Battalion assembled its
men in preparation for a break-out. One party of
fifteen men, including headquarters personnel, a
mortar section, and artillery observers, was trapped
in a group of houses 300 yards south of the caves.
After dark an attempt was made to relieve the
men and to clear a path through the enemy troops
blocking the route of escape. Only the latter objective was achieved. At 0130, shielded by a dark
night, Colonel Brown and his battalion, in column
of companies, slipped out of the caves and struck
south along the supply route toward the black-top
road which marked the final beachhead line. Capt.
Peter Graffagnino and his aid men elected to remain with the wounded, who had to be left behind.
The troops had covered almost half the distance
to safety when suddenly machine-gun and rifle fire
lashed out at them from a group of houses. The
men hit the ground and crawled for cover. The
column was split. Colonel Brown and the first half
of the column got through safely; the rest became
scattered. Smoke was laid down over the area and
in the early morning hours Captain Sparks and
Capt. George D. Kessler, the battalion S–3, managed to bring out part of the column. Small groups
continued to filter through during the day. Captain
Sparks was left without a single man in his Com-

pany E until two days later when Sgt. Leon Siehr
appeared. He had spent the last two days fighting
with the British. Of the original battalion only 225
men escaped and of this number 90 were hospital
cases. After a week of almost constant fighting
and nerve-shattering mortar and artillery fire, some
men had lost their hearing, others were barely
able to walk. For seven days and nights the battalion had fought off defeat. That any man returned is a tribute to the courage and stamina of
the American infantry soldiers who have made the
battle of the caves an epic of defensive fighting.

The relief of the 2d Battalion, 157th Infantry,
left the 2/7 Queens holding the caves and rolling
farmland immediately to the south. Efforts of the
2/6 Queens to get supplies through had failed
Even urgent requests for supply by air had to be
refused when stormy weather kept planes on the
ground. On 23 February enemy infantry supported
by tanks completed the work of sealing off the
already diminished battalion. Two companies were
overrun and a third was forced to withdraw into
the caves with the battalion headquarters. After
dark that night the remaining troops were divided
into groups of twelve to fifteen and an attempt
was made to infiltrate back to the positions of the
2/6 Queens. Few succeeded. The effort to hold
the former positions of the 2d Battalion, 157th
Infantry, had to be abandoned, and the enemy completed his occupation of the bulge in the western
shoulder of the salient.

The battle of the caves did not end the fighting
on the left shoulder. It was merely the most important and most costly action in a bloody war of
attrition in which whole squads and platoons disappeared without leaving a trace. The deep ravines
and rough nature of the country west of the Albano road made it impossible to develop a continuous line of defense or to employ artillery effectively against the enemy groups which infiltrated
between and into the positions of the defending
troops. All of the units of the 1 and 56 Divisions
holding the forward areas were tired and understrength; the units which were sent up to relieve
them were in the same condition. The 56 Division

reported on 25 February that its 167 Brigade was at only 35 percent of effective strength, the 168 Brigade at 50 percent, and the 169 Brigade, which had seen no action at the beachhead before 20 February, was down to 45 percent, not counting the 2/7 Queens, which had been reduced to 15 percent during the battle of the caves. Although the enemy's tactics of nibbling away at the left shoulder failed to carry him as far south as the vital lateral road, the drain on the strength of the British divisions was becoming more serious daily.

At the same time that the bitter struggle on the left shoulder of the salient was in progress, the enemy launched attacks in lesser strength against the right shoulder. (Map No. 18.) Late in the afternoon of 20 February enemy infantry attempted to infiltrate the positions of Lt. Col. James M. Churchill's 3d Battalion, 180th Infantry, covering the road leading north from the village of Padiglione, and of Company F, 1st Battalion, 180th Infantry, astride La Ficoccia Creek. Intense concentrations of enemy artillery fire preceded and accompanied the attacks. At noon three tanks of Company H, 1st Armored Regiment, protecting the bridge across Spaccasassi Creek, were damaged by the shelling; in the afternoon the remainder of the company and a platoon of Company I engaged the enemy tanks and infantry attacking the 180th Infantry. A bitter tank battle ensued before the enemy armor was driven off, and the 1st Armored Regiment suffered such heavy losses that the remaining tanks of Companies H and I were consolidated under the control of Company H. To guard the infantry against a possible armored breakthrough, that night engineers, protected by troops of Company L, 180th Infantry, destroyed the bridge over Spaccasassi Creek. Two Germans, captured by the infantry, reported that they had been sent forward with a similar order to blow the vital bridge.

On the morning of 21 February and again late in the afternoon the enemy continued his attacks against the right shoulder of the salient. Dive bombers and a 30-minute concentration of airburst antiaircraft fire preceded the afternoon attack. As on the previous day the infantry action was on a minor scale compared to the bloody battles of 16–19 February, but the artillery fire was the heaviest yet experienced at the beachhead. Occupying an exposed position near the blown bridge, 2d Lt. Walter F. Russell used his M–4 tank as a forward observation post. Pounded by the tank guns and by the accurate artillery fire called for by Lieutenant Russell (who was given a battlefield promotion the next day), the enemy tanks and infantry withdrew at dusk. That night, in an effort to renew the attack on the morning of the 22 February, the enemy assembled a force of approximately four hundred men, including elements of the *1st* and *2d Battalions, 1028th Panzer Grenadier Regiment,* the *741st Infantry Regiment,* and the *114th* and the *Hermann Goering Reconnaissance Battalions.* The variety of units represented and the relatively small size of the total force was proof that the enemy was having trouble finding troops to throw into the battle. The 180th Infantry called for defensive fires which so effectively covered all stream beds and avenues of approach that the enemy withdrew without making contact.

2d Lt. Jack C. Montgomery, a platoon leader of Company I, 180th Infantry, saw to it that not all of the enemy returned. Two hours before daylight he detected troops moving into the no man's land directly in front of his platoon. Armed with a rifle and several grenades Lieutenant Montgomery crawled up a ditch to within a few yards of the nearest enemy position where the Germans had set up four machine guns and a mortar. Then, climbing onto a little knob, he fired his rifle and pelted the surprised Germans with hand grenades until he had killed eight men, and the remaining four in the position had surrendered. After returning with his prisoners and reporting to the artillery the location of a house where he suspected the main enemy force was concentrated, Lieutenant Montgomery picked up a carbine and started back up the shallow ditch. Locating a second position he silenced 2 machine guns, killed at least 3 of the enemy, and took 7 more prisoners. Although it was now daylight and the open fields offered no concealment, Montgomery refused to relinquish his role of one-man army. As soon as the artillery had finished firing on the house he had spotted as a strong point, he rushed forward and rounded up 21 stunned Germans to bring his total for the morning to 11 dead, 32 prisoners, and an unknown number of wounded. Against resistance of this kind the enemy gained little ground on the sector of the front held by the 180th Infantry. The effort to gnaw away the right shoulder of the salient was given up.

While the attacks on the shoulders of the salient were in progress, General Mackensen proceeded with the regrouping and reinforcement of *Fourteenth Army* units in preparation for a new major drive against the beachhead. Before the attack in the Albano road sector had ground to a standstill, the enemy had committed his reserve divisions, the *26th Panzer* and *29th Panzer Grenadier,* in the areas previously held by the *3d Panzer Grenadier* and *715th Infantry Divisions.* In preparing for the new offensive, the *29th Panzer Grenadier Division* was withdrawn into *Army* reserve, and the *26th Panzer Division* was shifted to the Cisterna front. By the time that the Germans launched their new attack on the 3d Division front on 29 February, the Albano road sector south and west of the Factory was again occupied by the *65th Infantry* and *3d Panzer Grenadier Divisions,* both of which had received replacements and new attachments; the command of *I Parachute Corps* was extended to include these divisions, and its boundary with *LXXVI Panzer Corps* was now situated near the shoulder of the salient southeast of the Factory.

For the new assault, German divisions under the command of *LXXVI Panzer Corps* were arranged as follows, in order from Spaccasassi Creek eastward to the Mussolini Canal: the *114th Light Division,* facing southeast toward Carano, and reinforced by the attachment of the *1028th Panzer Grenadier Regiment* (formerly with the *715th Infantry Division*); the *362d Infantry Division,* a newly organized unit initially engaged in coast-watching near the mouth of the Tiber, which was filled out with new units transferred from the Adriatic front; the *26th Panzer Division,* in position west of Ponte Rotto; and the *Hermann Goering Panzer Division,* before Cisterna. Units under the command of the *715th Infantry Division* were also located at the eastern end of the front. With the *4th Parachute Division,* which commanded the Moletta River line, *Fourteenth Army* had 9 divisions facing the 5 divisions of VI Corps, and 5 of the German divisions had been concentrated for an assault on the U.S. 3d Division. (Map No. 19.) The enemy divisions were considerably understrength, however, and there was no great disparity in numbers between the opposing Allied and German forces.

The initial objective of the impending German drive was to penetrate the outer beachhead defense positions on a line running from Carano to Isola Bella. Depending on the success of the first day's attack, the enemy then planned to push toward the west branch of the Mussolini Canal—the final Allied beachhead defense line. If the attack developed successfully, *Fourteenth Army* planned to commit the reserve *29th Panzer Grenadier Division* to bolster the assault of the advancing German forces, either on the west flank along Spaccasassi Creek or in a surprise attack against the 3d Division right flank to be launched from east of the main Mussolini Canal.

On the eve of the German attack of 29 February, the forward positions of the 3d Division extended from a point one mile west of Carano to the junction of the west branch with the main Mussolini Canal. The outer defense line was held by the following units, in order from west to east: the 509th Parachute Infantry Battalion, with the attached 3d Battalion, 30th Infantry, on the left, occupied the forward line on either side of Carano; the 7th Infantry, the line from Formal del Bove Creek to Ponte Rotto; the 15th Infantry, from Ponte Rotto through Isola Bella to a position just west of Cisterna Creek; and the 504th Parachute Infantry, with the attached 4th Ranger Battalion on the left, from Cisterna Creek to the Mussolini Canal and thence to its junction with the west

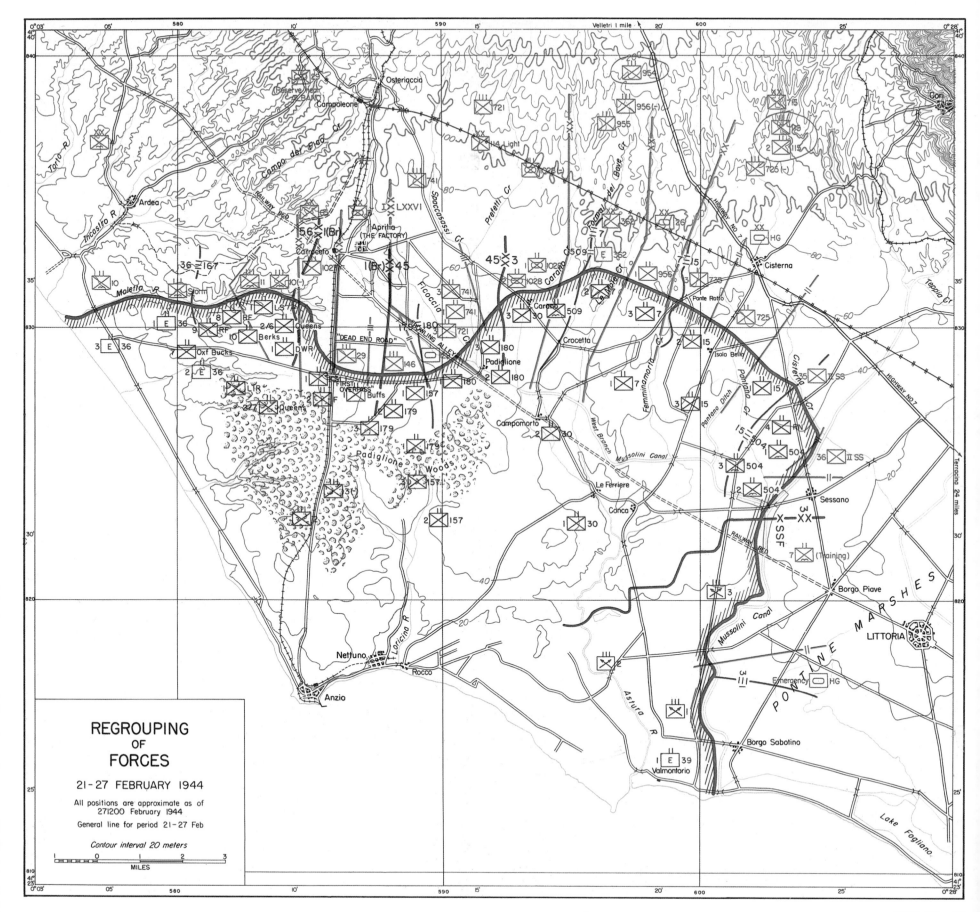

REGROUPING
OF
FORCES

21–27 FEBRUARY 1944

All positions are approximate as of
271200 February 1944

General line for period 21–27 Feb

Contour interval 20 meters

MILES

*MAP NO. 19*

branch. Each regiment in the forward line had one or more battalions in reserve, and the bulk of the 30th Infantry was also held in reserve. (Map No. 19.) Because of the relaxation of enemy pressure against the western half of the beachhead front after 25 February, VI Corps had ample reserves to reinforce the 3d Division in case the enemy seriously threatened to break through its positions.

The regrouping of Allied forces after the Germans had been stopped on 20 February was accompanied by a change in the command of VI Corps. The former commander of the 3d Division, General Truscott, who had been named Deputy Commander of VI Corps on 17 February, succeeded General Lucas as Commander of VI Corps on 23 February. General Lucas returned to the United States, where he subsequently became Commanding General of the Fourth Army.

## The 3d Division Repulses the Enemy

On the afternoon of 28 February the enemy laid down a smoke screen on the front of the 3d Division to conceal last-minute troop movements. After midnight enemy artillery fire shifted from the British front to the 3d Division sector, paying special attention to the village of Carano. VI Corps, anticipating the attack on the 3d Division, had matched the shift of enemy guns to the east by moving the 27th and 91st Armored Field Artillery Battalions to the vicinity of Conca where they could thicken the fire of the 3d Division artillery. At 0430, Corps and division artillery responded to the enemy fire with an hour-long counter preparation which blasted the enemy front-line positions and assembly areas. For every shell that cratered the muddy ground or struck a farmhouse within the American lines, VI Corps' massive array of guns threw back twenty. The Germans estimated that Allied artillery fired 66,000 rounds of ammunition on 29 February, more than double the number fired on any single day in the big offensive of 16–20 February. Artillery alone could not stop the attack. Just as the first streaks of dawn glinted on the snow-covered peaks of the Lepini Mountains

MAJ. GEN. LUCIAN K. TRUSCOTT
*Commanding General, VI Corps*
*(23 February 1944)*

smoke began rolling in on the 3d Division front. A few moments later 3d Division artillery observers were calling frantically for fire missions as one choice target after another presented itself. Striking at half a dozen points along the front, enemy infantry and armor surged forward against the 3d Division defenses. (Map No. 20.)

Of the enemy's initial attacks only the one directed against the sector of the 509th Parachute Infantry Battalion achieved any appreciable success. For this attack the enemy assigned the *1028th Panzer Grenadier Regiment* the mission of taking the village of Carano, and elements of the *362d Infantry Division* were to reach the road junction a mile and one-half southeast of Carano. Engineer troops were to assist the assault waves in opening gaps through the outer defenses.

The principal attack struck Company B, 509th Parachute Infantry, which was dug in on a low hill a mile northeast of the village of Carano.

When artillery fire began falling on the company area, 1st Lt. John R. Martin, the company commander, called for counterbattery and defensive fires from the supporting artillery and the 83d Chemical Battalion's 4.2-inch mortars. Enemy shells knocked out the telephone lines to the battalion and all firing had to be done without observation. Before dawn, company outposts spotted the first wave of gray-green troops advancing through the smoke screen. The little group on the hill held its fire, waiting for the enemy to come within range. The smoke was beginning to lift now and the defending troops could see more clearly. Suddenly, as enemy assault engineers, equipped with wire cutters and bangalore torpedoes, began cutting paths through the shell-torn barbed wire, the hill erupted in a sheet of flame. Rifle and machine-gun bullets tore gaps in the advance wave of the attackers. The Germans faltered, then pushed on. Singing and shouting they swarmed up the slope and rushed the positions of the greatly outnumbered paratroopers. When the enemy closed in on the company command post, the executive officer, in the absence of Lieutenant Martin, who was believed to have been wounded, ordered the remnants of the company to withdraw. Only one officer and twenty-two men reached the

battalion's main line of resistance some 700 yards to the rear. The rest of the company was listed as missing in action, though many men were killed in the final hand-to-hand struggle for possession of the hill.

Having broken through the initial beachhead line of resistance the troops of the *1st Battalion, 1028th Panzer Grenadier Regiment,* who led the assault, swung southwest across the open fields lying between Carano Creek and Formal del Bove Creek, which ran through deep ravines leading south toward the west branch of the Mussolini Canal. Advancing on a 1,000-yard skirmish line, the enemy closed in on the paratroopers of Company A who were dug in north of the road below Carano. At 0735, Lt. Col. William P. Yarborough, the battalion commander, tried to get a call through requesting air support. The line to the rear was out. When the 7th Infantry, on the right, sent a platoon of its supporting tanks to assist, muddy fields held them up. It was left to the artillery, the mortars, and the ninety-six men comprising Company A to stop the attack. Division and Corps artillery were now zeroed in on the attacking troops, and the paratroopers 81-mm. mortar platoon and three 60-mm. mortars located along the Carano road fired with deadly effect,

SMOKE OVER THE FRONT LINES *was the prevalent condition during the Anzio campaign as one force or the other prepared for an attack. This picture, taken from a farmhouse observation post, shows the zone of a German attack and obscures the Lepini Mountains beyond.*

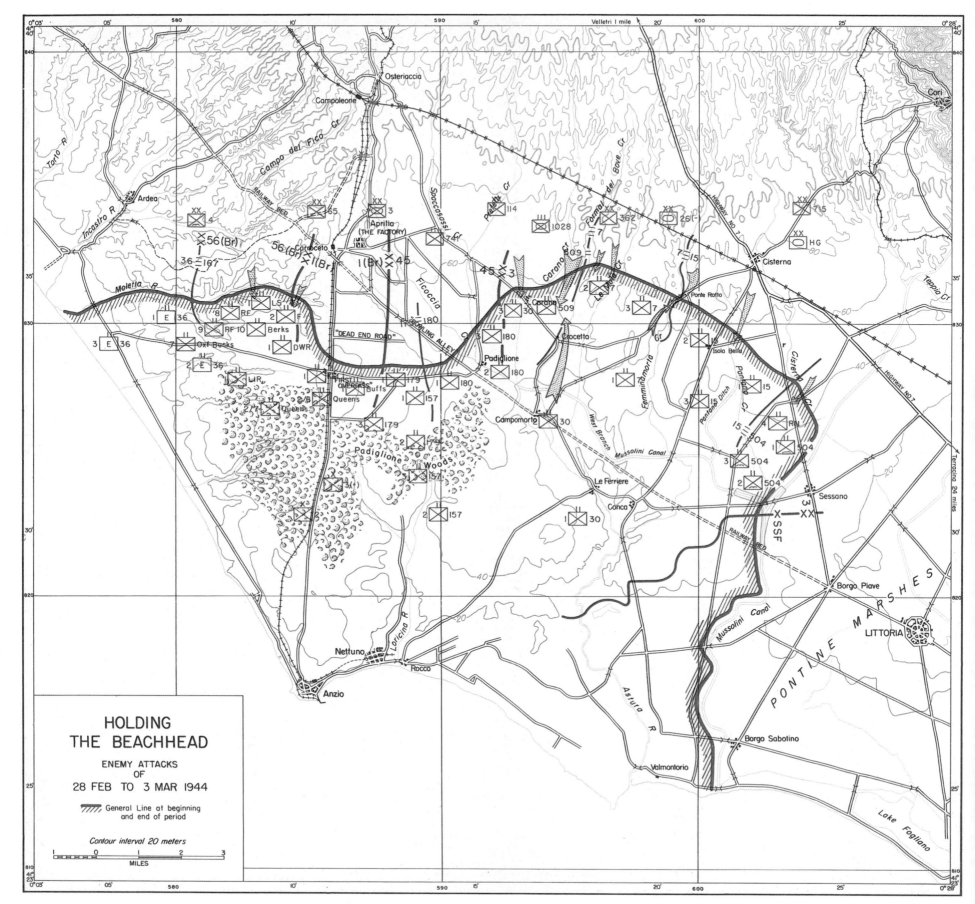

HOLDING
THE BEACHHEAD

ENEMY ATTACKS
OF
28 FEB TO 3 MAR 1944

General Line at beginning
and end of period

Contour interval 20 meters

MILES

MAP NO. 20

until the enemy got so close that the mortar men had to reach for their rifles. Under fire from all sides the enemy force stopped short of the road and sought cover in the ditches. It had penetrated 800 yards to the intermediate beachhead line, but the enemy needed to widen his narrow salient if he was to capitalize on his initial success.

Simultaneous enemy attacks to gain ground on the flanks of the salient failed. West of Carano the assault parties of the *2d Battalion, 1028th Panzer Grenadier Regiment,* attacking at 0530, became tangled in the wire in front of Company I, 30th Infantry. Before they could cut their way through, machine-gun fire killed a German officer, and twenty-one of his men surrendered. At 0630 the attack was repeated. Again a German officer was killed and eighteen more of the enemy surrendered. Tank and infantry attacks against Company L, 30th Infantry, were broken up by artillery fire and a platoon of the 751st Tank Battalion. Sgt. William Bolich had concealed his tank in a house where he could cover the road into Carano. While he was observing from the turret, an enemy shell struck the house bringing down part of the stone and masonry wall. Sergeant Bolich was struck in the back by a piece of concrete and a second block damaged the elevating mechanism of the 75-mm. gun so that the muzzle could not be raised. In spite of his injured back, Sergeant Bolich crawled out of the turret and propped up the barrel of the gun sufficiently to allow the gunner to fire. In the course of the day the damaged M–4 knocked out three Mark IV tanks and effectively stopped the armored attack.

East of Carano the troops of the *362d Infantry Division* tried repeatedly but unsuccessfully to deepen and widen the salient that had been won between Carano Creek and Formal del Bove Creek, directing their attacks against the 2d Battalion, 7th Infantry. In each case massed Corps and division artillery fire broke up the infantry drives, while supporting tanks and tank destroyers held off the enemy armor. Mortar fire systematically searched the deep ditches which the enemy used as routes of approach and as protection against the artillery.

During the morning of 29 February the Allied air effort was nullified by heavy clouds and squalls, but beginning at 1500 247 fighter-bombers and 24 light bombers bombed and strafed enemy tanks and infantry close behind the lines. In the attacks on the west flank of the 3d Division front which had begun at daylight, the Germans had gained some ground but were unable to exploit their penetration. Although communication within American units was poor, individual positions remained secure. The danger of a breakthrough on the division left appeared to be over. At 1930 the 2d Battalion, 30th Infantry, and a platoon of Company C, 509th Parachute Infantry Battalion, launched a counterattack to regain the lost ground.

East of the Carano sector, other troops of the *362d Infantry Division* attempted to penetrate between the positions of the 2d and 3d Battalions, 7th Infantry, along the axis of Le Mole Creek. Making use of the dirt roads leading south through the rolling country between the ditches, enemy tanks in groups of three to six supported the infantry. One platoon of Company G was overrun by tanks and Colonel Sherman had to commit elements of the reserve 1st Battalion. Small-scale but bitter fighting raged all along the front as the opposing forces struggled to gain control of strategic farmhouses or knolls. Colonel Sherman's troops held their ground and at the end of the day the *362d Infantry Division* had little to show for its efforts.

Farther to the east the *26th Panzer Division* had better success. Mark IV and Mark VI Tiger tanks attacked the 3d Battalion's right flank west of Ponte Rotto. Striking at noon down the Cisterna–Campomorto road the tanks and armored infantry drove Company L back from a bridge 1,000 yards southwest of Ponte Rotto. Lt. Col. William A. Weitzel, the 3d Battalion commander, sent a platoon of Company I forward to assist Company L, and the advance was checked. Late in the afternoon *nebelwerfer* rockets screamed into the 3d Battalion's positions and smoke covered the area as the *26th Panzer Division* attempted unsuccessfully to exploit its gains. General O'Daniel and

Colonel Sherman immediately took steps to deal with the danger of an armored breakthrough. After dark, engineers were ordered forward to mine and crater the road, tank destroyers and antitank guns were sent up, and artillery and mortar fire was concentrated on the enemy tanks. The 81-mm. mortars, in addition to their role of holding off the enemy infantry, had already accounted for two of the tanks, but so long as the enemy retained control of the captured bridge the threat of renewed attacks remained.

For his attack on the 15th Infantry, which held the ground on both sides of the Conca–Cisterna road, General Mackensen employed elements of the *Hermann Goering Panzer Division*. Before dawn a patrol of forty to fifty men infiltrated to the east of Isola Bella. It managed to get through the barbed wire and mine fields without being detected, and by daylight it was well within the outer beachhead defense line. There it was trapped and during the day the scattered enemy troops were mopped up before they could do any damage. The principal threat came from enemy tanks operating down the roads from Cisterna and Ponte Rotto. The tanks carried personnel for the purpose of clearing the roads of obstacles; otherwise, infantry played only a slight part in the attack. Company G, covering the battered village of Isola Bella, was under tank fire all day. Just before noon one platoon was driven out of its positions and at the end of the day the company was reduced to thirty-eight men with another twenty-five in the attached Company H, although others found their way back during the night. Company F was sent up to assist it and the key position of Isola Bella was held. The enemy's efforts to keep his tanks hidden in smoke only partly succeeded and the destroyers of the 601st Tank Destroyer Battalion had a field day. They knocked out at least seven of the attacking tanks and damaged nine others.

Enemy units under the command of the *715th Infantry Division* also launched diversionary attacks against the right flank of the 3d Division near the Mussolini Canal. In the sector of the 504th Parachute Infantry a composite company made up of elements drawn from the *715th Engineer Battalion* and the *16th SS-Reichsfuehrer Division* attacked at dawn to capture a bridge across Cisterna Creek. The 4th Ranger Battalion broke up the attack. Farther to the south *Combat Group Schindler*, made up of odds and ends of the *715th Infantry* and *Hermann Goering Panzer Divisions*, attempted to gain a bridgehead across the Mussolini Canal south of the village of Borgo Sabatino. Engineers carrying light foot ladders for use as bridging equipment led the advance. A strong patrol from the 1st Special Service Force laid an ambush in the no man's land on the east side of the canal and when the surprised enemy troops, many of whom were young and inexperienced boys, took refuge in a group of houses, artillery fire was concentrated on them. Thrown into confusion by the shelling, the enemy troops scattered. By midafternoon General Frederick's patrols, whose raids into enemy territory had for days kept their opponents terrorized, rounded up 4 officers and 107 men.

At the end of the first day of his offensive the enemy had hardly dented the 3d Division's outer line of defense. His tactic of attacking on a wide front with infantry units of company and battalion size, probably dictated by the open nature of the terrain and respect for VI Corps superiority in artillery, had broken down against the well-organized positions of the 3d Division troops. His armor, although more successful than the infantry, was hampered by mine fields and the ever-present mud which made it almost impossible to operate off the roads. Employed in small groups, the enemy tanks and self-propelled guns lacked the power necessary to achieve a breakthrough and they made good targets for VI Corps' emplaced tanks and tank destroyers. In the course of the day twenty-one enemy tanks were reported destroyed.

In holding off the enemy attacks the forward battalions of the 3d Division suffered heavy losses. They were forced to commit their reserve companies to back up the line, and individual companies from regimental reserves were drawn upon for local counterattacks. Nevertheless, with the exception of the commitment of the 2d Battalion, 30th

Infantry, to regain the ground lost northeast of Carano, the drain on division and Corps reserves was slight. Since it was estimated that the enemy still had available a considerable reserve of tanks, General Truscott attached to the 3d Division an additional company of tank destroyers and the 3d Battalion, 1st Armored Regiment. Orders also were issued that all roads leading into the beachhead should be cratered and new mine fields laid. With a large air support program promised, the 3d Division faced the second day of the enemy's offensive in a spirit of confidence.

The pattern of the enemy attacks on 1 March followed closely that of the preceding day, but on a reduced scale; their effectiveness was lessened by the vigorous countermeasures which General O'Daniel had taken to strengthen his positions. The counterattack launched by the 2d Battalion, 30th Infantry, late in the afternoon of 29 February, made good progress until the early morning hours of 1 March, when it was held up by enemy troops dug in around a house east of Carano. The battalion stopped to reorganize and then continued the attack at dawn, bypassing the point of resistance and pushing on to reach its objective, the former outpost line of the 509th Parachute Infantry Battalion, by 0830. Seventy-six prisoners were taken and an enemy counterattack repulsed during the morning. Before the enemy could launch a large-scale attack early in the afternoon, the battalion had consolidated its positions. Eighteen battalions of artillery were concentrated on the counterattacking enemy troops and their attack broke down. By dawn of 2 March the 30th Infantry had relieved all elements of the 509th Parachute Infantry Battalion, which then passed into division reserve. The enemy's hard-won gains on the 3d Division left flank had been erased.

The principal action on 1 March centered around the captured bridge southwest of Ponte Rotto. Efforts made by the 7th Infantry during the night of 29 February–1 March to destroy the enemy tanks at the bridge failed. Bazooka squads were stopped by enemy infantry protecting the bogged-down tanks and when, at General O'Daniel's suggestion, an attempt was made to illuminate them with flares so that the tank destroyers could fire, pouring rain ruined most of the flares. At 0345 Company K, astride a dirt road northwest of the bridge, was attacked by tanks and infantry. The tanks rolled right into the company lines and blasted the men from their fox holes, virtually annihilating one platoon. As all of their bazookas were out of order the men fought back with Molotov cocktails and sticky grenades. Artillery came to their support and the attack was stopped. At dawn the enemy shifted the emphasis to Company L near the bridge. The steady rain, which kept Allied planes on the ground, likewise hampered the movement of the enemy armor, already hemmed in by road craters and mine fields, and the attacks against the 7th Infantry as well as similar armored and infantry attacks against the 15th Infantry near Isola Bella, failed to gain any ground. General Truscott expressed his satisfaction in the progress of the battle when he told General O'Daniel he was "delighted with the way you have stopped the Boche."

Clear weather on 2 March permitted the Mediterranean Allied Air Force to carry out the extensive air program planned for the preceding day. It was an impressive display of Allied air power. Two hundred forty-one B–24 Liberators and 100 B–17 Fortresses, with 113 P–38 Lightnings and 63 P–47 Thunderbolts providing top cover, dropped thousands of fragmentation bombs on areas around Cisterna, Velletri, and Carroceto. The total of 351 heavy bombers was even greater than that flown on 17 February, the peak day in the air support given to VI Corps during General Mackensen's big drive. An equally impressive force of medium, light, and fighter-bombers concentrated on enemy tanks, gun positions, and assembly areas, particularly along the railroad running through Cisterna and Campoleone which served the enemy both as a final defense line and an assembly area from which to launch his attacks. The combined effect of the tremendous weight of bombs dropped during the daylight hours of 2 March and night bombing of the roads around Cisterna aided materially in dissuading the enemy from continuing the offensive.

Ground action on 2 March was on a limited scale. West of the Albano road the enemy resumed his tactics of infiltration on the front of the 1 and 56 Divisions and he launched one tank and infantry attack down the road to Isola Bella. In all cases the attacks were beaten off. At Ponte Rotto enemy engineers were busy constructing a bridge across Femminamorta Creek in an effort to salvage tanks which had been damaged or stuck in the mud and to open a way for a continuation of the attack on the 7th Infantry. Colonel Sherman's troops also were trying to get at the German tanks. A knocked out M–4 blocked the road making it impossible to get antitank guns forward. In the morning a bazooka squad managed to get close enough to throw Molotov cocktails at a tank. Three hits from a bazooka bounced off without damaging it and two Molotov cocktails were equally ineffective when they failed to catch fire. After dark the men tried again with more success. One tank was set afire and bazookas scored five hits on a Tiger tank. Artillery and tank destroyers had already disposed of at least four others. The stretch of road between the captured bridge and Ponte Rotto was becoming a graveyard of enemy armor. At Isola Bella enemy tank recovery crews tried to reach a damaged Ferdinand tank destroyer and a Tiger tank. Flares were shot over the area and the 601st Tank Destroyer Battalion saw to it that the damaged vehicles were still there the next morning.

At dawn on 3 March the enemy renewed his attack on the 3d Battalion, 7th Infantry, southwest of Ponte Rotto. Tanks and armored infantry of the *26th Panzer Division* broke through Company L's positions astride the road, forcing a slight withdrawal. Then the battalion held, and in the afternoon the 3d Division switched to the offensive. Colonel Sherman sent Company A, under Captain Athas, and Company B, under Maj. Lloyd B. Ramsey, up the road toward Ponte Rotto to recapture the contested bridge and restore the 7th Infantry's former positions. The division artillery poured smoke shells into the area ahead of the troops before the attack was launched at 1330. Some of the smoke drifted over beyond Ponte Rotto, giving the

15th Infantry the impression that it was the enemy who was preparing to attack. The 15th Infantry expended a lot of ammunition laying down defensive fires across its front until a call to 7th Infantry headquarters clarified the situation. The smoke was thin at first, then it improved and the two companies moved forward. Company B, attacking on the north side of the road, reached its objective northwest of the bridge without difficulty; two platoons of Company A, attacking along and to the south of the road, reached the crater where the engineers had created a road block. There they were met by tank fire and a terrific concentration of artillery. Captain Athas was killed and when the two platoons withdrew to reorganize only thirty men were left. Although the enemy still held the contested bridge, the counterattack served its purpose of stopping the enemy attack. At Isola Bella the 15th Infantry sent one company to regain the ground which had been lost on the first day of the enemy attack. No opposition was encountered and the former positions were reoccupied.

The counterattacks launched by the 3d Division on the afternoon of 3 March marked the end of the enemy's third and last major assault against the Anzio beachhead. It was a costly failure for the Germans. Their losses were heavy, both in personnel and equipment; in five days of fighting, 29 February–4 March, they suffered more than 3,500 battle casualties, and at least 30 of their tanks were destroyed. In this final attack, the Germans had made no further progress in reducing the size of the beachhead; their penetrations in the 3d Division outpost line of defense were almost wiped out by Allied counterattacks. Their units had sustained heavy losses and the lack of adequate replacements rendered the *Fourteenth Army* for the time being incapable of further large-scale offensive action.

The troops of VI Corps were also approaching the point of exhaustion. Six weeks of almost continuous bombing, shelling, and bitter fighting, first to extend the beachhead and then to hold off the enemy attacks, had taken a terrific toll in lives and energy. Fortunately the 3d Division, which bore the brunt of the last enemy offensive, had been given

ENEMY LOSSES *in equipment and personnel were high in the attacks of 29 February–3 March. Above: A mine-sweeping detail is clearing the area around destroyed German Mark IV tanks. Below: Prisoners are loaded onto an LCI at Anzio, enroute to a prison camp. Some prisoners were Russians previously captured by the enemy.*

an opportunity to prepare for the final German attack. The weeks when the enemy was concentrating his assaults along the axis of the Albano road had been used to absorb and train replacements and to strengthen defenses. As General Mackensen learned to his cost, the beachhead forward line of defense had been developed into a well-integrated and formidable barrier. When the enemy attack lost its momentum, the 3d Division, although weakened, was still capable of sustained fighting and its positions were almost intact.

The situation in the British sector of the beachhead improved as the enemy weakened. The arrival on 2 March of the 9 and 40 Royal Marine Commandos with a total strength of 660 men provided a force of fresh and highly trained troops. Assigned to the 56 Division, the Commandos were employed in raids along the fluid front west of the Albano road. The tactics of guerilla warfare, which the enemy employed so successfully while he retained the initiative, were now turned against him. The situation was further improved when the British 5 Division moved to the beachhead during the second week of March and relieved the weakened 56 Division.

Field Marshal Kesselring sent a message to General Mackensen at 1840 on 1 March ordering that the assault against the 3d Division be halted, and that offensive operations be limited to local counterattacks. *Fourteenth Army* relayed these orders to its subordinate units, and the last major enemy drive against the Anzio beachhead came to an end. The enemy attributed the failure of his final drive to bad weather and to the poor condition of the assaulting troops. Four days of intermittent rain (27 February–1 March) had bogged down enemy armor, and it seemed pointless to continue the costly infantry attacks without armored support. A more important explanation of the enemy failure, in the opinion of the commander of the *Fourteenth Army,* was the inadequate training of units received as reinforcements, the youth and inexperi-

ence of replacements, and the general depletion and exhaustion of the attacking forces after the previous weeks of heavy fighting. At a German High Command conference on 3 March, the enemy decided to abandon, at least for the time being, all plans for further major offensive operations on the Anzio front. On 4 March, *Fourteenth Army* issued an order to its units instructing them to hold their present positions and to develop them defensively as quickly as possible. The German High Command had given official recognition to a situation already apparent to its troops: the enemy efforts to destroy the beachhead had failed.

The enemy had started his offensive in a spirit of confidence and with the determination to make any sacrifice necessary to victory. He had drawn upon his dwindling reserves in northern Italy, France, Yugoslavia, and Germany to build up an effective striking force. Then he attacked. His first drive, designed to pave the way for the breakthrough, was launched with skill and aggressiveness, and he won his objectives. In the period 3–10 February the Campoleone salient was wiped out, and the Factory and Carroceto were taken. He had then massed his forces for the blow which he expected would carry his infantry and armor through to the sea. In the crucial struggle of 16–20 February, the beachhead line of defense bent, but did not break. Although the enemy attempted to continue his offensive and to pour more troops into the battle after 20 February, he was unable to make up his losses or restore the confidence of his troops. His attacks during the last drive launched on 29 February showed both timidity and lack of coordination. The enemy's efforts to win a victory which would bolster flagging morale at home and restore the reputation of the German Army abroad had broken down against the stubborn resistance of the Allied troops holding the Anzio beachhead; they had brought him only a further depletion of his already strained resources in equipment and manpower.

# THE BREAKTHROUGH

After the repulse of the German attack on the 3d Division, the character of the fighting at Anzio underwent a radical change. For nearly three months, VI Corps and *Fourteenth Army* limited their operations to an active defense of the positions they held at the conclusion of the German offensive. The Allied and enemy forces in the Anzio area were marking time, awaiting the renewal of Allied offensive operations on the southern front. Both forces engaged in aggressive patrolling. The Allied Air Force and VI Corps artillery constantly pounded enemy positions, and the enemy retaliated with medium and long-range artillery fire and air raids against Allied shipping and supply dumps. After drafting plans for renewing his offensive against the beachhead, the enemy decided to conserve his depleted combat strength for the big Allied drive to come. VI Corps built up its forces and accumulated a huge supply reserve in preparation for the great May offensive which was to carry the Fifth Army through to Rome.

Adjusting itself to its new defensive role, the *Fourteenth Army* regrouped its forces by reducing the number of units occupying the perimeter of the beachhead front. During March, the *Hermann Goering Panzer Division* was sent north to Leghorn for rest and refitting; the *114th Light Division* was transferred to the Adriatic front; and *Fourteenth Army's* two best divisions, the *26th Panzer* and *29th Panzer Grenadier,* were withdrawn to the area south of Rome as *Army* reserves. These two divisions were subsequently designated as *Army Group* reserves, making them available for action against an Allied offensive in the south, a new at-

tempt of VI Corps to break out of the beachhead, or a new Allied landing in the enemy rear above Anzio. Some replacement units arrived at the beachhead, including two battalions of Italian troops that were employed east of the main Mussolini Canal in the Littoria sector. The Germans displayed little confidence in their Axis partners, brigading them with German formations down to alternate platoons in the line and at night taking over the positions held by Italian troops.

The enemy regroupings substantially reduced the combat strength of the forces holding the beachhead perimeter; in early April, only the reinforced *3d Panzer Grenadier Division* was rated as having first-class combat quality. But the total number of *Fourteenth Army* troops was greater in mid-March than during the February offensives. As of 14 March, it reported a strength of 135,698, a total which included about 65,800 German combat troops; by 10 April, this combat strength had increased to 70,400.

The enemy seriously considered a renewal of offensive operations at Anzio. Tentative plans drafted on 13 March provided for a large-scale attack to be launched on 29 March either in the Albano road sector or from Cisterna. On 23 March the date of the projected attack was postponed, and it was abandoned altogether on 10 April. Field Marshal Kesselring was reluctant to commit his best reserves, the *26th Panzer* and *29th Panzer Grenadier Divisions,* in a renewed offensive at Anzio; without them, General Mackensen judged that a large-scale attack could not succeed. When the Allies finally launched their spring offensive along the southern front on 11 May, the enemy was forced to strip the *Fourteenth Army* of its reserves in order to check the Allied advance. Thus, when VI Corps joined in the offensive on 23 May, the forces opposing it had been greatly weakened.

Fifth Army also undertook an extensive program of regrouping and reinforcement of VI Corps units at Anzio. Among British units, the 56 Division, which had been rushed to Anzio in the criticals days of February, was relieved by the 5 Division in early March and left the beachhead. The British Commando units were also withdrawn. The 1 Division remained at Anzio, except for the 24 Guards Brigade which was sent to Naples to reorganize; it was replaced by the 18 Brigade. Of the American units, only the paratroopers and Ranger Force left the beachhead. The 504th Parachute Infantry, long overdue to rejoin the 82d Airborne Division, left for the United Kingdom late in March; on 1 April the 509th Parachute Infantry Battalion also departed. These losses were more than offset by the arrival of new units, notably the

A DESTROYED AMMUNITION DUMP *in the beachhead area, hit by German long-range artillery. Although this stack of about 25 tons of 105-mm. ammunition was destroyed, the explosion was kept from spreading by the earthen revetments which protected every supply pile.*

veteran 34th Division; this division, which began to disembark on 21 March, relieved the 3d Division on the Cisterna front on 28 March, after the latter had completed sixty-seven consecutive days of front-line duty. The arrival of 14,000 replacements in March brought Allied units up to full strength. By the end of the month the numerical strength of the combat units of VI Corps was equal to that of six full divisions—approximately 90,000 men—and considerably exceeded that of the opposing *Fourteenth Army*.

VI Corps, like the enemy, at least contemplated a resumption of the offensive during March. Preliminary plans for a large-scale operation in the Albano road sector were issued on 11 March. A definite plan was outlined in Field Order No. 18 of 18 March. It proposed a frontal assault by the British 1 and 5 Divisions against the German salient astride the Albano road; meanwhile the American 45th Division was to attack from the southeast toward the Factory. The 5 Division was to continue its attack along the old railroad bed which ran northwest from Carroceto. The 45th Division, in cooperation with the 3d Division striking from the east, was to follow through by capturing the Factory and Carroceto. The 1st Armored Division would then pass through the 1 Division up the Albano road and exploit the advances of the infantry. Other projects for offensive operations were issued in April for planning purposes, but there seems to have been no serious intent of putting them into effect. VI Corps as well as the enemy awaited the renewal of the offensive in the south. In the meantime, it limited its operations to patrolling and local attacks designed to keep the enemy on the defensive.

The description of some of a typical day's operations and events may serve to illustrate the weeks of relative inaction at Anzio. Before dawn on 15 April, eight enemy aircraft dropped antipersonnel and high explosive bombs in the areas of the 1 Division and 1st Armored Division. They struck an ammunition dump and a gasoline dump, and caused a few casualties at the 1st Armored Division command post. Antiaircraft shot down one of the

enemy planes and probably destroyed another. At 0530, the 2d Regiment of the 1st Special Service Force, supported by twelve tanks of the 1st Armored Regiment, launched a raid on the village of Cerreto Alto, southwest of Littoria; after seizing this objective and other enemy positions in the vicinity, the raiding force withdrew at 1115. Sixty-one enemy prisoners, including seventeen Italians, were captured. The attacking force suffered only one casualty but lost two medium tanks. Elsewhere along the front the situation remained unchanged. Enemy artillery fire was somewhat lighter than on preceding days, and the usual long-range firing of heavy enemy guns did not occur. American artillery fires were directed against enemy tanks and self-propelled guns in front of Isola Bella; and in the afternoon the newly introduced 240-mm. howitzers destroyed several enemy-occupied buildings in the vicinity of Cisterna. On the British front, mortars were used to scatter enemy troops working on fixed defenses. During the day, Allied planes flew ninety-nine sorties in the VI Corps area, somewhat fewer than normal. Behind the lines, 3,513 tons of supplies were unloaded, slightly above the average daily total of 3,191 for April. Total combat casualties of VI Corps on 15 April were 105 (20 killed, 83 wounded, and 2 missing), slightly below the daily average of 107.5 for April.

## The Problem of Supply

The Anzio landing of VI Corps as originally conceived was to be the prelude to a short-term operation that would lead to a quick junction with an advancing main Fifth Army. When that advance failed to materialize, the initial plans for supplying the beachhead had to be radically revised and expanded. Supplies were brought in by preloaded trucks on LST's, by LCT's, and on Liberty ships. Beginning on 28 January, a convoy of six LST's was dispatched daily from Naples, each vessel carrying fifty preloaded trucks. Each convoy brought in a 1,500-ton load, 60 percent of which was ammunition, 20 percent fuel, and 20 percent rations. Fifteen LCT's also made a weekly turnaround from

A RAID ON AN ENEMY POSITION, *as seen in these four pictures, was typical of operations in the weeks of relative quiet at Anzio. Above: A 1st Special Service Force detachment attacks the position. Below: Rifle fire keeps the enemy down as the team moves closer.*

RUSHING THE FARMHOUSE *after the German defenders had been seen leaving the buildings (above) and, finally, soldiers in the house pouring machine-gun fire into a haystack after the last enemy had been either killed or forced to retreat across the field.*

Naples with supplies. Every ten days four Liberty ships, loaded with supplies at Naples or at North African ports, were scheduled to arrive at the beachhead. The LST's and LCT's could dock in Anzio harbor, while the Liberty ships had to be unloaded off shore and their cargo brought into the harbor or over the beaches by LCT's or (in calm weather) directly by DUKW's. Since VI Corps was not equipped to handle supply functions, Fifth Army assumed control of the port and dump areas on 6 February. The 540th Engineers took over the operation of the port and beaches, and their commanding officer, Col. George W. Marvin, became port commandant.

As the whole beachhead area was within range of observed enemy artillery fire and subjected to constant air raids, a difficult and unique supply situation prevailed at Anzio. Enemy artillery and air attacks endangered beach and dock personnel and reduced their efficiency by an estimated 10 percent. Since ammunition and gasoline dumps were of necessity concentrated in a small and highly vulnerable area, some material damage also occurred. Between 22 January and 10 March, 1,043.8

tons of ammunition were destroyed by enemy bombing and 228.5 tons by artillery fire, an average of 27.7 tons per day. But material losses were at no time critical. Supplies were dispersed in many separate dumps and protected by earthen bunkers erected by bulldozers and Italian laborers. To help in this work, the 16th Armored Engineer Battalion improvised an armored bulldozer by mounting a bulldozer blade on an M–4 tank. As time went on, VI Corps counterbattery fires, improved air defenses, and bombing attacks on enemy gun positions reduced the effectiveness of enemy bombing and shelling of supply areas.

At the end of January the security of the beachhead was threatened by ammunition and labor shortages. For a time, the Corps' most valuable counterbattery weapon (the 155-mm. howitzer) had to be limited to twenty-five rounds per gun per day, but gradually the supplies of ammunition were replenished and reserves built up. The beachhead needed many civilian laborers to clean up debris and to dig in dump areas. Soon after the landing, the bulk (about 22,000) of the civilian population was evacuated from the beachhead, and only about

A SUPPLY DUMP *in the Anzio area is screened from enemy observation by smoke laid down by the 179th Chemical Smoke Co. A few of the stacks have been revetted, and others are dispersed widely to minimize damage from enemy artillery and air bombardment.*

ANZIO ANNIE, *a German 280-mm. railroad rifle of the type employed during the latter part of the Anzio campaign. When the Allied breakthrough occurred, the enemy moved this piece to Civitavecchia, where it was knocked out by American air attacks.*

750 able-bodied civilians were left available for work. To alleviate the labor shortage Italian workers were recruited in Naples and brought to Anzio. At first a port battalion was stationed at the beachhead to unload Liberty ships. About 1 March a new practice was adopted of placing a port company on board each Liberty ship at Naples, and having it return with the vessel to Naples. The opportunity for a quick departure from the dangerous Anzio area was an incentive to rapid unloading.

A shortage of LCT's, needed to unload Liberty ships, developed at the beginning of February. Most of these craft had been in service for more than a year without overhaul and they frequently broke down. On 6 February only fifteen were avail-

able, a number that was increased to twenty-two by 12 February. As a stop-gap, from ten to twenty LCI's were successfully employed in unloading supplies. An effort was made to persuade the Liberty ships to come in closer to shore so that they could be unloaded directly by DUKW's, but ship captains were reluctant to do so in the face of heavy shelling. Between 450 and 490 DUKW's were in use at Anzio. The craft situation greatly eased at the end of February, when sufficient LCT's again became available.

By March, supply problems at the beachhead had been largely solved. With improving weather and adequate craft for unloading, it was possible to discharge five or six Liberty ships at a time. The proportion of supplies unloaded from Liberty ships greatly increased; by May they were discharging six times as much cargo as the LST's. The greatest volume of supplies came in during the month of March, when 157,274 tons were discharged; on the peak day, 29 March, 7,828 tons were unloaded. Large reserves were built up in anticipation of the Fifth Army's resumption of the offensive. By 23 May the beachhead had, in addition to its normal 10-day reserve, a month's additional reserve of supplies. Between 22 January and 1 June, 513,511 long tons of supplies were discharged at Anzio, the over-all daily average being 3,920 tons. As a result of careful planning and efficient operation, supply never became a critical problem at Anzio.

## Life at the Beachhead

From the beginning of March the forward positions at Anzio beachhead were stabilized and remained practically unchanged until the breakthrough in May. Conditions at Anzio resembled the quiescent periods of trench warfare on the Western Front during World War I. The great

VI CORPS HEADQUARTERS AT NETTUNO *occupied extensive wine cellars under the town. Carved out of solid rock, the cellars were safe from even the heaviest enemy bombardment.*

bulk of VI Corps casualties were caused by enemy air raids and especially by enemy artillery fire. The narrow confines of the beachhead made it peculiarly vulnerable to enemy artillery, which ranged from 88-mm. guns up to giant 280-mm. railroad guns. One of the latter was popularly known as the "Anzio Express," also as "Anzio Annie." These big guns, not to be confused with the smaller railroad guns which the Germans had employed during February, were first reported in action on 24 March. During March, 83 percent of the combat casualties of the 3d Division were caused by shell fragments, although the division occupied a long sector of the forward line until the end of the month. VI Corps' highly centralized fire control center carried out a systematic program of counterbattery firing to combat enemy artillery. Its efforts became more effective in April with the arrival at the beachhead of heavier artillery weapons—8-inch guns and howitzers and 240-mm. howitzers.

Smoke generators, used to create an artificial fog behind the lines, helped to reduce the accuracy of enemy artillery and of bombing; but there was only one effective answer to the problem of security from the constant pounding of enemy shells and bombs: that was to go underground. The whole beachhead area became a honeycomb of trenches, fox holes, and dugouts as the men burrowed into the sandy ground. Bulldozers dug pits for guns and vehicles and pushed up tons of earth around the neatly stacked piles of gasoline cans and ammunition which were located in every open field in the rear areas. During the rainy winter months the process of digging in was hampered by the proximity of the ground water to the surface. Fox holes and dugouts quickly filled with water. With the arrival of spring, warm and sunny days dried up the ground and it became possible to construct a dugout without striking water. Viewed from the air the beachhead created the illusion that thousands of giant moles had been at work.

In the American hospital area near Anzio, the 36th Engineers set to work excavating foundations three and one-half feet deep for hospital tents; the sides of each tent were further strengthened by sandbag walls. Even with these improvements, the hospital area remained one of the more dangerous spots on the beachhead. No soldier who was at Anzio will forget the work of the doctors, nurses, and aid men who served with them. When the shells were coming over or the air raid siren signalled a red alert others could seek shelter; the doctor performing an operation or the nurse tending a patient had no choice but to continue in the performance of his or her task. A measure of their courage and willingness to sacrifice themselves for their patients is indicated by the losses suffered by medical personnel at the beachhead. Ninety-two were reported killed in action (including 6 nurses), 387 wounded, 19 captured, and 60 reported missing in action.

VI Corps headquarters was initially located in the Hotel de Ville at Nettuno. After this building was struck by shells and bombs, the headquarters was established in caverns which the inhabitants had used for wine cellars. This was a popular spot while the wine lasted, but men tied to desk jobs in the little cubbyholes off the narrow corridors soon felt that they were sealed for life in catacombs. After the Fifth Army Advanced Command Post was established at the beachhead, it was located in a tunnel beneath Villa Borghese on the hill above Anzio harbor. Other troops built their own shelters. Wooden beams, doors, scrap lumber, and huge wine barrels from destroyed farmhouses, together with hundreds of thousands of sandbags and ammunitions boxes, were consumed in the construction of tiny underground homes. The barrels, sunk deep in the ground, made good bedrooms if one could stand the odor of stale wine. In any event, protection was more important than comfort.

To counteract the debilitating effects of static warfare, General Truscott not only conducted a vigorous training program but also endeavored to give his men as much rest and recreation as possible when they were out of the line. Owing to the open nature of most of the beachhead terrain, troops in forward areas usually stayed underground during the day; at night combat patrols probed deep into the enemy lines, and occasionally a company or battalion launched an attack to take prisoners or capture or destroy a strategic group of buildings. Recreation and training facilities were limited by the lack of a safe rear area. The 1st Armored Division built two underground theaters, each capable of holding over two hundred men. Each division set up small recreation and bath units; at the latter, the men could obtain a complete change of clothing. On the coast below Nettuno the 3d Division established a large rest camp where men could combine training with opportunities for swimming, going to the movies, and writing letters. Every four days VI Corps sent 750 men by LST to the Fifth Army rest camp at Caserta. Troops at the beachhead were given priority on mail, Post Exchange supplies, and recreation equip-

ment. The quality of their food also improved. During February rear-area as well as front-line troops lived almost exclusively on C and K rations; by March calmer seas and lessened enemy activity permitted Liberty ships to bring in fresh meat and a high percentage of B rations.

Where organized recreation was impossible, men provided their own amusement. Horseshoes were in great demand, and volley ball and even baseball games were played close to the fighting front. When enemy shells started coming in, the men ducked for cover and then calmly returned to their games. A few troops had their own chicken pens; others, less fortunate, dickered with the few remaining Italian farmers for eggs. Patrols for chickens and livestock were as carefully planned as patrols against the enemy. To help pass the long hours in dugouts men improvised radio sets on

REVETTING THE HOSPITAL TENTS *at the beachhead. This photo shows three phases of construction. First (far left), a burlap retaining wall is set up; second (center), earth is packed around the outside; third and, (right), a ward tent is erected over the revetment. A newsreel photographer records the construction of this evacuation hospital.*

LIVING CONDITIONS AT THE FRONT *during the latter part of the Anzio campaign were much improved as the men protected their fox holes with sandbags, tarpaulins, and camouflaged roofs. Fighting was light and living was leisurely, disturbed only by sporadic shelling and bombing.*

which they could listen to the Fifth Army Expeditionary Station and also to Axis propaganda broadcasts. "Sally," the German radio entertainer, was as well known to them as the "Anzio Express." They enjoyed her throaty voice and her selections of the latest American popular music; they laughed at her crude propaganda and that of her partner "George," just as they laughed at the German propaganda leaflets which they collected for souvenirs. German efforts to sow discontent among the Allied troops at the beachhead were singularly unsuccessful. They merely supplied an additional source of entertainment.

It was easy for a replacement arriving at the beachhead on one of the beautiful spring days of April or early May to gain the impression that, despite all the evidence of destruction around the tiny harbor, Anzio was a relatively safe spot. Even the occasional white plume of water, rising as an enemy shell plunged into the calm bay, had an impersonal air about it. Men worked at the docks unloading LST's or LCT's, drivers of DUKW's churned their vehicles out across the bay toward the Liberty ships outside the harbor, antiaircraft crews lolled by their guns, and a few men swam along the shore below the battered villas. But the apparent unconcern of the men was deceptive. The terrific tension under which they had lived during the critical days of February had eased somewhat, but some measure of it was still there. The next shell to whistle over the beachhead might well land in the hold of a ship or obliterate a truck driving through the streets of Anzio or Nettuno. At dusk the feeling of tension increased; men around the harbor kept an eye on the end of the jetty, where the raising of a flag gave warning of another air attack. Although the enemy abandoned daylight raids after the costly attacks of February, anywhere from one to half a dozen attacks were made every night, and the enemy shelling, sporadic during daylight hours, substantially increased after dark. One night at Anzio dispelled all illusions of security. The battle of the beachhead remained a grim and deadly struggle to the end.

## Casualties

Both VI Corps and the enemy suffered heavy losses in combat casualties during the four months between the Allied landing at Anzio on 22 January and the attack out of the beachhead on 23 May. In presenting casualty statistics, a note of caution is in order. Since it is impossible to compile an exact record of combat casualties for any large-scale operation, those presented here should be treated as an approximation.

The combat casualties of VI Corps at Anzio through 22 May numbered about 30,000, including at least 4,400 killed and 18,000 wounded in action. Of these totals, American units lost approximately 17,000 men, including at least 2,800 killed and 11,000 wounded in action. The enemy reported the capture of 6,800 Allied prisoners, including about 2,400 American troops. About two-thirds of the combat casualties occurred during the period of heavy fighting that ended on 3 March. During the first thirty days of the Anzio operation, the combat casualties of VI Corps amounted to about 17 percent of its effective strength. British combat losses were relatively heavier than American, in terms of the number of troops engaged; during the above 30-day period, their units lost 27 percent of their

effective strength. In addition to the combat losses, VI Corps reported over 37,000 noncombat casualties during the whole period of the Anzio operation, more than 26,000 of whom were American. About 33,000 casualties, combat and noncombat, were evacuated by sea from Anzio—including 24,000 Americans—without the loss of a single patient's life as a result of the process of moving men from shore hospitals to the waiting ships.

*Fourteenth Army* lost between 28,000 and 30,000 men as combat casualties in its operations against the Anzio beachhead. This total included at least 5,500 killed and 17,500 wounded in action. The Allies captured more than 4,500 enemy prisoners of war. The German combat losses during the period of relative inaction after 3 March were about 10,000, almost exactly the same as those of the Allied forces.

The total combat casualties of VI Corps and *Fourteenth Army* were thus roughly equal, although the enemy had a larger number of troops killed in action. Three factors made the enemy losses relatively more costly in terms of combat strength than those of the Allies. The Germans suffered higher losses among combat units, they received far fewer replacements than Allied units, and the replacements they did receive were of progressively poorer quality.

## The Breakthrough, 23 May–4 June

On the night of 11–12 May, main Fifth Army launched its spring offensive against the Gustav Line in the south. (Map No. 2.) After the failure of the Cassino assaults in February, the Fifth Army boundary had been moved southwestward toward the coast, and the British Eighth Army took command on the Cassino front. In the new offensive, Fifth Army attacked from its bridgehead north of the Garigliano into the hill masses between the Liri Valley and the sea; while the Eighth Army, heavily reinforced, at the same time launched its attack on the Cassino front. Cassino and the dominant mountains to the north fell only after a week of heavy fighting, and the Eighth Army pushed

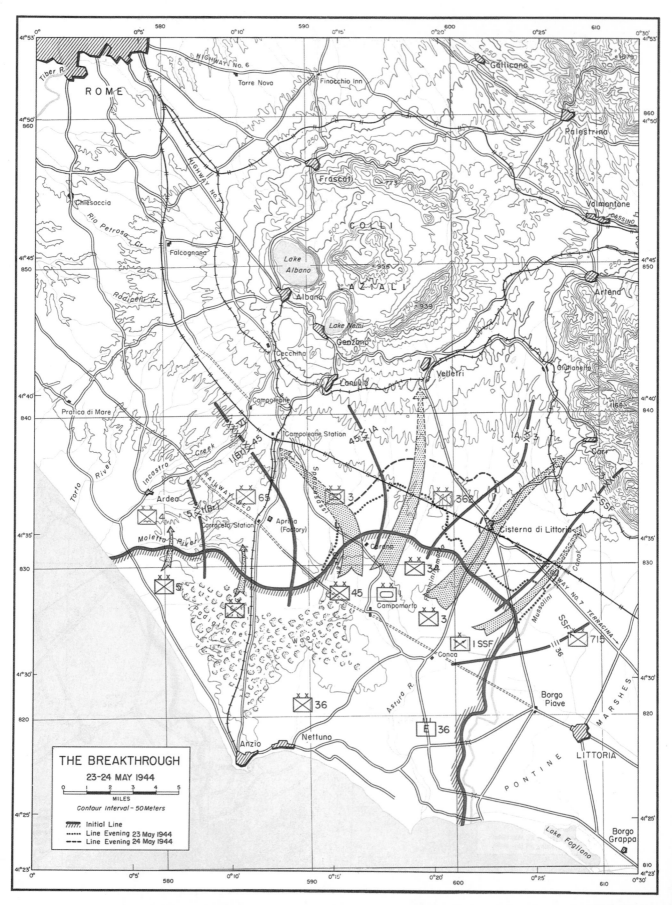

THE BREAKTHROUGH
23-24 MAY 1944

0 1 2 3 4 5
MILES

Contour Interval - 50 Meters

Initial Line
Line Evening 23 May 1944
Line Evening 24 May 1944

on slowly up the Liri Valley against strong German opposition. Meanwhile, after three days of stubborn fighting, Fifth Army's two corps—the French Expeditionary Corps on the right, and II Corps on the left along the coast—broke through the Gustav Line positions and started the rapid drive northward that was not to be halted until Rome was entered on 4 June.

As late as 15 May, General Clark had under consideration a plan to shift the two divisions of II Corps (the 85th and 88th) by sea to Anzio after they had completed their initial breakthrough in the south. They were to have combined with VI Corps to conduct a powerful drive out of the beachhead. But the pace of the advance in the south promised to collapse the German coastal defenses and permit a quick juncture between II and VI Corps by land. On 20 May, therefore, General Clark directed II Corps to continue its attack toward Terracina, situated at the southern end of the coastal plain that extended northwestward to the Anzio beachhead. Terracina fell on the night of 23–24 May. American troops then raced northward over the flat land of the Pontine Marshes to meet the 1st Battalion, 36th Combat Engineers (Task Force Brett), which had advanced south from the beachhead. The junction was effected at 0731 on 25 May, and General Clark (who had moved to Anzio to direct the offensive) personally greeted his men from the south at 1020. Anzio was a beachhead no longer; it was now the left flank of the main fighting front.

During the first eleven days of the spring offensive, the character of the Anzio front remained unchanged; but behind the forward lines, the forces of VI Corps were busily preparing for their part in the big Allied drive. To strengthen the beachhead forces, early in May Combat Command B had joined the 1st Armored Division, which was now at full strength. On 22 May, the day before the attack out of the beachhead, the 36th Division landed at Anzio; this brought the strength of the beachhead forces to seven full divisions together with a large number of auxiliary supporting units. VI Corps had prepared three different plans for an

attack out of the beachhead; on 5 May, plan BUFFALO was adopted to govern the Anzio offensive. However, to deceive the enemy, preparations for all three plans were carried out. Essentially, plan BUFFALO projected a breakthrough on the Cisterna front toward Cori at the base of the Lepini Mountains and Velletri at the base of Colli Laziali; the attack would then continue through the Velletri Gap to Valmontone in order to cut Highway No. 6, the main supply route of the German *Tenth Army*. The initial assault was to be launched through the front held by the 34th Division, with the 1st Armored Division advancing on the left, the 3d Division in the center (directly toward Cisterna), and the reinforced 1st Special Service Force on the right. On the left flank the 45th Division was to penetrate beyond Carano as far as the Campoleone–Cisterna railroad. The 36th Division, after its arrival, was earmarked to exploit a breakthrough. The British 1 and 5 Divisions, holding the western end of the beachhead front, were to launch local attacks to deceive the enemy as to the main course of the beachhead offensive and to contain enemy forces that were opposing them. (Map No. 21.) The British divisions were detached from VI Corps and reverted to Fifth Army control on 22 May, the day before the attack.

Until the Fifth and Eighth Armies began their offensive on 11–12 May, the German *Fourteenth Army* had substantially maintained its strength. The *26th Panzer* and *29th Panzer Grenadier Divisions* had become *Army Group* reserves, but they were kept in the area south of Rome and were available for use against an attempted Allied thrust out of the beachhead. Then came the breakthrough in the south, and Field Marshal Kesselring was forced not only to commit his *Army Group* reserves but also to strip *Fourteenth Army* of its combat reserves to bolster the hard-pressed *Tenth Army*. General Mackensen protested, but his protests were overruled until it was too late to stem the American advance out of the beachhead. In anticipating the Allied spring offensive, the enemy made two major miscalculations, revealed in an estimate of the Allied situation drafted on 30 April. The Ger-

THE CAPTURE OF CISTERNA *came as the beachhead forces linked up with American troops advancing from the south. Many prisoners were found in the battered ruins (above) and hustled to the rear. From the air (below), Cisterna appeared as nothing but a gutted pile of rubble.*

mans believed (and continued to believe as late as 20 May) that Fifth Army would make a new seaborne landing, either between Anzio and the southern front at Gaeta or Terracina, or (less probably) to the northwest of Anzio near the mouth of the Tiber River. In view of this belief, Field Marshal Kesselring was reluctant to release his reserves or strengthen the German forces in the immediate vicinity of Anzio until the very eve of the Anzio offensive. The second German miscalculation—natural enough, in view of the preceding offensives—was that VI Corps would launch its main assault up the Albano road past the Factory. Thus the better German divisions—the *65th Infantry* and *3d Panzer Grenadier*—continued to occupy the Albano road sector; while the Cisterna and Mussolini Canal sectors were held by the weaker *362d* and *715th Infantry Divisions*. When the attack came on 23 May, the enemy was unable to shift his strength to the Cisterna sector.

At 0545 on 23 May, a tremendous Allied artillery barrage was directed against the enemy defenses along the Cisterna front. Forty-five minutes later, American tanks and infantry emerged from the smoke all along the front from Carano to the Mussolini Canal to launch the assault. At first, the enemy resistance was stiff, and German mine fields took a heavy toll of American tanks and tank destroyers; but before noon, the 1st Special Service Force had cut Highway No. 7 below Cisterna, and all units had reached their initial objectives. Bad weather curtailed the planned air support, but before the day was over 722 missions had been flown; Cisterna and more distant objectives were heavily bombed. By evening, the 1st Armored Division had crossed the Cisterna–Campoleone railroad, and had smashed the enemy main line of resistance.

The enemy estimated that, by the end of the first day's attack, the *362d Infantry Division* had lost 50 percent of its fighting power, and two regiments of the *715th Infantry Division* had been badly mauled. The *Hermann Goering Panzer Division* was rushed southward from Leghorn; and *Fourteenth Army* planned to detach combat units from *I Parachute Corps,* holding the Moletta River–Al-

bano road sector, to bolster the shattered forces of *LXXVI Panzer Corps* on the Cisterna front. This step was frustrated by the holding attacks of the British 1 and 5 Divisions and the attack on the left flank by the 45th Division. General Mackensen realized his precarious position, but his request to withdraw his left flank to the base of the Lepini Mountains was refused.

Resuming the attack on 24 May, VI Corps troops drove forward beyond the railroad to cut Highway No. 7 above Cisterna, and virtually to encircle Cisterna itself. On 25 May the German defenses to the rear of Cisterna crumbled, and Cisterna itself fell to the troops of the 3d Division, who collected nearly a thousand enemy prisoners. By nightfall, 3d Division and 1st Special Service Force units were at the base of the Lepini Mountains, before Cori; meanwhile, 1st Armored Division troops had reached a position halfway between Cori and Velletri, thus facing the entrance of the Velletri Gap leading toward Valmontone. On 26 May, the 1st Armored Division advanced to within two miles of Velletri; while the 3d Division raced through the Velletri Gap its reconnaissance units reached the outskirts of Artena, only three miles from the goal of Valmontone and Highway No. 6. Although Artena was captured on the following day, the VI Corps advance then came to a temporary halt. The plans for the continuation of the Fifth Army's attack were being recast, and the enemy had now somewhat recovered from his confusion. In particular, elements of the *Hermann Goering Panzer Division* had reached the Valmontone area and were counterattacking the *3d Division.* (Map No. 22.)

VI Corps' highly successful offensive out of the Anzio beachhead was nevertheless costly in losses, both in men and material. In the first five days of the attack, combat casualties exceeded 4,000; they were almost twice as heavy in killed and wounded as during the five days of the big German attack of 16–20 February. The 1st Armored Division and other armored units supporting the infantry lost at least eighty-six tanks and tank destroyers in the first day's attack alone. Enemy losses were far heavier; no figures are available for the number of enemy troops that were killed and wounded, but in the first five days of the attack VI Corps captured 4,838 prisoners and, among items of enemy material, destroyed or damaged more than 2,700 motor transports.

On 26 May General Clark issued new orders to VI Corps which reshaped the nature and direction of its attack. Hitherto, the main axis of advance had been toward Valmontone; now, the weight of the VI Corps drive was to be shifted to the west of Colli Laziali, to seize a line from the Factory through Campoleone to Lanuvio. (Map No. 23.) The 34th Division would advance northwest from below Velletri (which was stubbornly defended by the enemy) toward Lanuvio, while the 45th Division attacked toward Campoleone Station. Initially, the 1st Armored Division was allotted the task of attacking Velletri; subsequently (28 May) it was shifted to the left flank to strengthen the attack of the 45th Division. In the Artena area, the 3d Division was to continue its advance on Valmontone, while the wide gap between the attacks to the west and east of Colli Laziali was to be plugged by the 36th Division. This general plan was carried out in the face of stiffening enemy resistance. The 45th Division drove to Campoleone village by 29 May, and the 34th Division reached the outskirts of Lanuvio on the same date. (Map

THE FALL OF THE FACTORY *came the morning of 28 May as British troops pushed northward through its still-burning ruins. The soldier at the right crouches against a wall, taking cover from a few enemy snipers still remaining in the wreckage.*

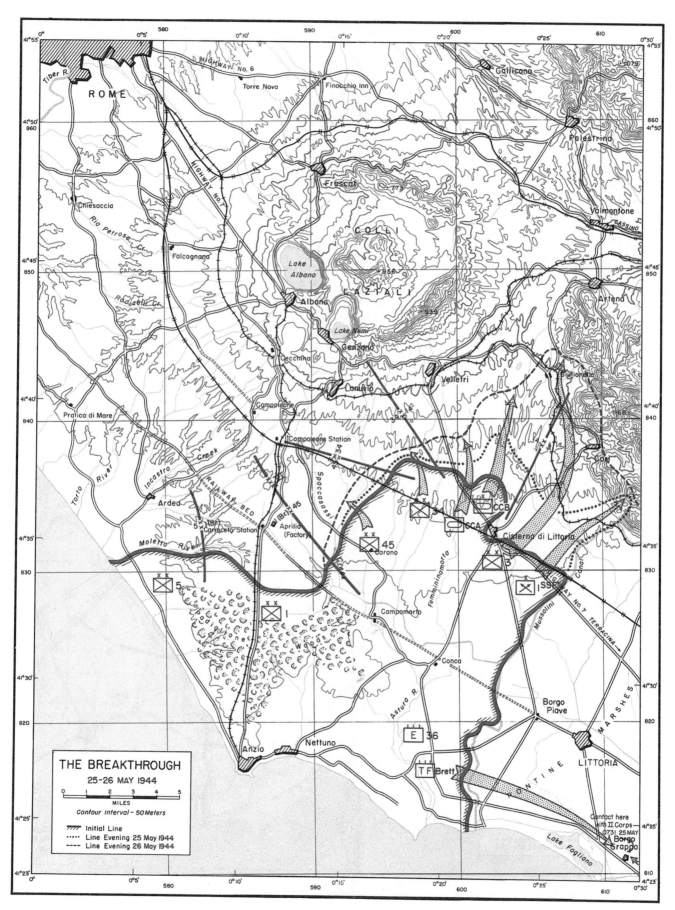

ROME

Tiber R.

HIGHWAY No. 6

Torre Nova

Finocchio Inn

Gallicano

Palestrina

CASSINO

Valmontone

Chiesaccia

Rio Petroso Cr.

HIGHWAY No. 7

Falcognana

Radicell Cr.

COLLI

Frascati

Lake
Albano

LAZIALI

Albano

Lake Nemi

Genzano

Arteno

Pratica di Mare

Cecchina

Lanuvio

Velletri

Giulianello

Campoleone

Creek

Ardea

Incastro

Campoleone Station

RAILWAY BED

Spaccasassi

Carroceto Station

Aprilia
(Factory)

Carano

CCB

Cisterna di Littoria

Moletta River

Campomorto

Femminamorta

SSF

HIGHWAY No. 7 TERRACINA

Mussolini Canal

Padiglione

Wood

Conca

Astura R.

Borgo
Piave

PONTINE

MARSHES

LITTORIA

Anzio

Nettuno

E   36

Borgo
Grappa

T F Brett

Lake Foglino

Contact here
with II Corps
0731 25 MAY

THE BREAKTHROUGH

25-26 MAY 1944

0  1  2  3  4  5
MILES

Contour Interval - 50 Meters

Initial Line
Line Evening 25 May 1944
Line Evening 26 May 1944

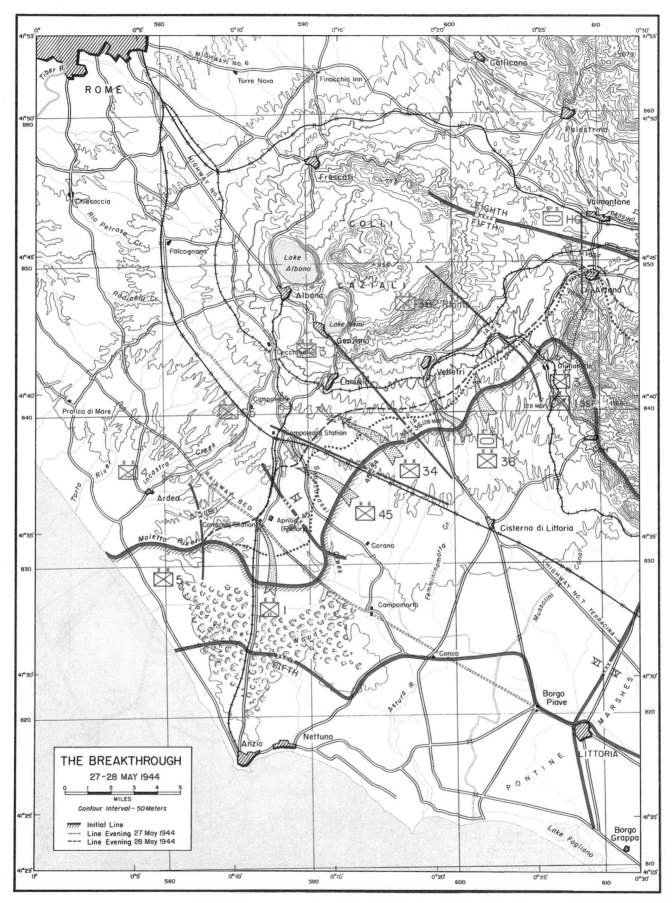

THE BREAKTHROUGH
27-28 MAY 1944

0 1 2 3 4 5
MILES

Contour Interval - 50 Meters

Initial Line
Line Evening 27 May 1944
Line Evening 28 May 1944

THE ENTRY INTO ROME *on 3 June climaxed months of bitter fighting at Anzio. Troops moving into the Eternal City found little trace of the fast-retreating enemy, and fired at only a few suspected positions.*

No. 24.) The 36th Division moved in before Velletri, but initially its role was limited to aggressive reconnaissance. In the east, the 3d Division was held on the defensive by the counterattacking *Hermann Goering Panzer Division.* On 30 May the 3d Division and 1st Special Service Force passed to the control of II Corps, which thereafter commanded the attack toward Valmontone and Highway No. 6.

The enemy had been hard pressed to round up sufficient troops to check the American advance. He had been forced to withdraw to a new defensive line, extending from Ardea near the coast through Lanuvio and Velletri to a position before Valmontone, and German units were ordered by Hitler to hold this line at all costs. In a change of Corps boundaries, *Fourteenth Army* assigned the sector west of Colli Laziali to *I Parachute Corps,* and the sector to the east to *LXXVI Panzer Corps.* In the reshuffling of units and the Corps boundaries, the mountainous region of Colli Laziali just east of Velletri was left temporarily almost denuded of enemy troops; the Germans had concentrated their depleted forces in defense of Lanuvio and Valmontone.

At dusk on 30 May the Fifth Army drive appeared to have been stalled. (Map No. 24.) On the left flank west of Colli Laziali, the 1st Armored Division and 45th Division had fought bitterly but unsuccessfully along the Albano road above Campoleone all day; and the attack of the 34th Division before Lanuvio had been stopped on 29 May. On the new II Corps front east of Colli Laziali, the 85th Division was just coming in to reinforce the 3d Division, which had remained on the defensive since 27 May. Actually, General Clark had been informed by General Truscott of the gap in the enemy defense line along the rugged base of Colli Laziali between the units of *I Parachute Corps* and *LXXVI Panzer Corps,* and he moved quickly to exploit this weakness. Late in the evening of 30 May, troops of the 36th Division (142d Infantry, followed by 143d Infantry) started to climb the steep slopes of Colli Laziali east of Velletri, undetected by the enemy. By dawn on 31 May, American troops had made a deep penetration that flanked both enemy corps, and not a shot had been fired to herald their advance. When the Germans discovered this dangerous penetration of their defensive line, they counterattacked; but the 36th Division held to its key positions which outflanked the main enemy line of resistance and permitted the advance on Rome to continue. (Map No. 25.)

Despite their now untenable positions, the separated corps of *Fourteenth Army* fought hard for three days (31 May–2 June) to check the Fifth Army's advance. Enemy resistance was especially stiff on the VI Corps front to the west of Colli Laziali. But when II Corps swept around the north of the mountains and the 36th Division reached the central heights of Colli Laziali, the enemy decided that the time had come to pull out. On the night of 2–3 June the main enemy forces hurriedly withdrew northward, leaving only scattered rear guards to impede the Fifth Army's advance into Rome. On 3 June all units of the Fifth Army hastened after the retreating enemy, and at 0800 on the morning of 4 June the first American troops reached the outskirts of Rome. Actual entry into the city was delayed until early afternoon when elements of the 1st Armored and 36th Divisions moved in simultaneously to occupy the Italian

capital. By the end of the day, Fifth Army troops held the entire south bank of the Tiber from the sea to the junction of the Tiber and Aniene Rivers above Rome. By the next evening, the tide of battle had rolled far beyond Rome, as Fifth Army pursued the fleeing enemy to its next line of mountain defenses.

With the capture of Rome, Fifth Army attained the ultimate goal toward which the Anzio landing had originally been directed. On the eve of the landing on 22 January, the Allied High Command had hoped that the surprise assault behind the German *Tenth Army,* combined with a strong offensive in the south, would collapse the enemy's resistance along the Gustav Line and lead to a rapid march on Rome. Actually, the Anzio assault did not become a phase in an over-all Allied offensive, for the attack in the south stalled on the very day that the men of VI Corps swarmed unopposed over the beaches near Anzio. What had been envisioned as a brief operation coordinated with an Allied drive from the south became an isolated and bitter struggle to preserve a strategic foothold far behind the main enemy line of defense. Reinforced, Allied VI Corps was able to hold the beachhead, and then to build up its forces to fulfill its role in the spectacular spring offensive. Operation SHINGLE was crowned with final success; the grim defense of the American and British troops who held the Anzio beachhead led to a victory that forecast the collapse of the German war machine and the triumphant conclusion of the Allied war effort.

☆ U.S. GOVERNMENT PRINTING OFFICE: 1990  249–158

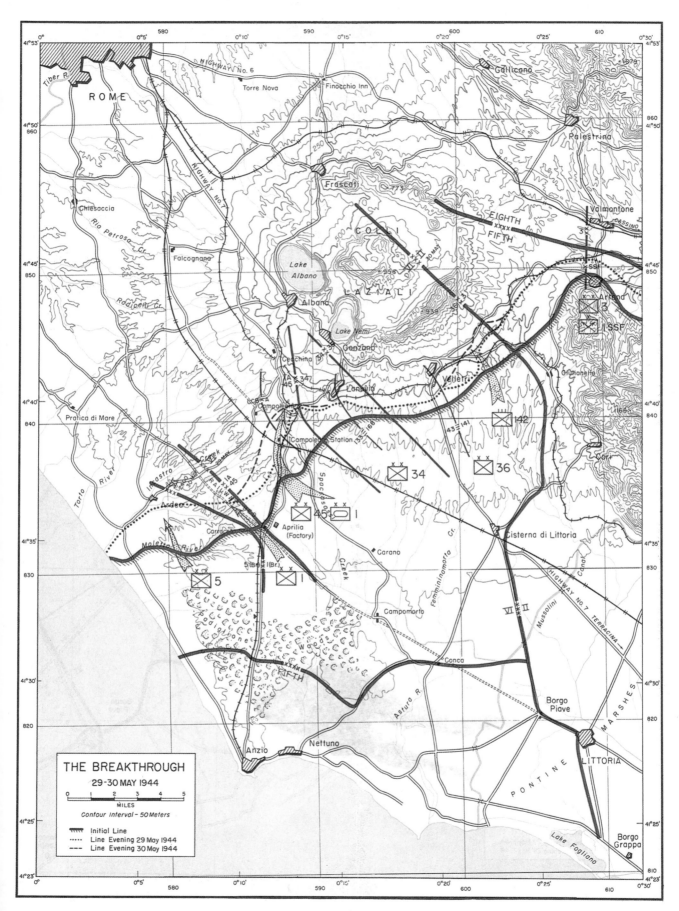

ROME

Tiber R.

HIGHWAY No. 6

Torre Nova

Finocchio Inn

Gallicano

Palestrina

Chiesaccia

Rio Petroso Cr.

HIGHWAY No. 7

Falcognana

Frascati

EIGHTH

FIFTH

Valmontone

CASSINO

SSF

Roaigeti Cr.

COLLI

Lake
Albano

LAZIALI

Albano

SSF

3

I SSF

Pratica di Mare

Ceccina

Lake Nemi

Genzano

Velletri

34

Lanuvio

Compoleone

142

45

Torto River

Incastro

RAILWAY

Ardea

Compoleone Station

Spaccasassi Creek

Carro

Aprilia
(Factory)

Garano

36

Cisterna di Littoria

Cori

Moletta River

5 (Br.) I (Br.)

I

Femminamorta Cr.

HIGHWAY No. 7 TERRACINA

5

Garano

Greek

Campomorto

VI II

Mussolini Canal

FIFTH

Padiglione Wood

Conca

Astura R.

Borgo
Piave

LITTORIA

PONTINE

MARSHES

Anzio

Nettuno

Borgo
Grappa

Lake Fogliano

## THE BREAKTHROUGH
### 29-30 MAY 1944

0 1 2 3 4 5
MILES

Contour Interval - 50 Meters

〰〰〰 Initial Line
········· Line Evening 29 May 1944
- - - - - Line Evening 30 May 1944

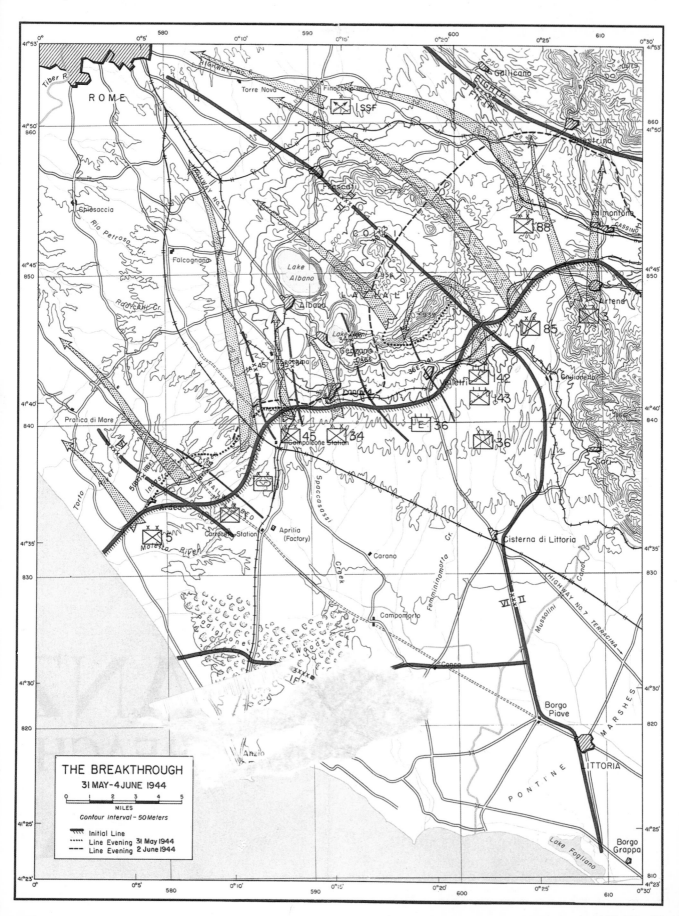

THE BREAKTHROUGH
31 MAY - 4 JUNE 1944

0  1  2  3  4  5
MILES

Contour Interval - 50 Meters

Initial Line
Line Evening 31 May 1944
Line Evening 2 June 1944

MAP NO. 25